The Optina Elders Series

ELDER ANTHONY OF OPTINA

ELDER ANTHONY OF OPTINA
Detail of a portrait in the main refectory of the
recently reopened Optina Monastery.

ELDER ANTHONY
of Optina

by
FR. CLEMENT SEDERHOLM

ST. HERMAN OF ALASKA BROTHERHOOD
1994

Address all correspondence to:
St. Herman of Alaska Brotherhood
P.O. Box 70
Platina, California 96076

Front cover: Line engraving by Natalia Kareva, Moscow, 1994

FIRST ENGLISH EDITION
Translated from the Russian edition: *Zhizneopisanie Nastoyatelya Maloyaroslavetskago Nikolaevskago Monastirya Igumena Antoniya [Biography of the Superior of Maloyaroslavets-St. Nicholas Monastery, Abbot Anthony],* published by the Kozelsk Optina Monastery of the Entrance of the Mother of God, Moscow, 1870. Second Russian edition: *Optinskii Starets Igumen Antonii, Zhizneopisanie i Zapisi [Optina Elder Abbot Anthony, Life and Writings],* published by the St. Herman of Alaska Brotherhood, Platina, California, 1973.

Library of Congress Cataloging in Publication Data

Sederholm, Fr. Clement
    Elder Anthony of Optina.
    Translated from the Russian.

Library of Congress Catalogue Card Number: 94-065658
ISBN 0-938635-51-4

Dedicated to the memory
of a distant Optina disciple,

ARCHIMANDRITE VLADIMIR

on the fifth year of his repose.

Never having seen Optina,
he was a disseminator of its tradition.

Icon of the Synaxis of the Optina Elders.
Icon painted by Monk Andrew in honor of their canonization.

Bottom row, left to right: Saints Moses, Anthony, Ambrose,
Leonid (Lev), Macarius and Hilarion. *Middle row:* Saints Anatole,
Barsanuphius, Joseph and Isaac. *Top row:* Saints Nikon, Nectarius,
Anatole the Younger and Isaac the Younger.

CONTENTS

Fr. Vladimir, a distant disciple of the Optina Elders. Pascha, 1959.

INTRODUCTION

A Gift of Optina to America

ON THE BICENTENNIAL OF ORTHODOXY
IN AMERICA

THE BOOK you are holding in your hands is a translation of the original *Prima Vita* of Elder Anthony, one of two founders of the famous Optina Monastery in Central Russia. It was authored by his disciple, a convert from Lutheran Protestantism, Fr. Clement Sederholm, and published only a few years after the Elder's death. Since Elder Anthony was one of the founding fathers of Optina, his biography was used in his monastery as one of the major building blocks for the spiritual life of each novice who sought spiritual formation. Thus, the book originally had a special purpose, and was more than just an ordinary biography of a righteous man. Likewise, the second printing of the original Russian version, as well as the present English translation, also has a special purpose: to form spiritually hungry American souls into conscientious inheritors of the heavenly treasure of Optina, and to give beginners in the spiritual life a tool with which to chisel a life worthy of a true Christian out of the mess of contemporary barbarism.

Elder Anthony of Optina is closely linked with America. The first Orthodox Mission from Valaam Monastery in Russia arrived 200 years ago on the soil of the American continent, with St. Herman of Alaska among the missionaries. In spite of the worldliness of the pioneers and fur traders *(promyshlenniki)*, St. Herman made an attempt to infuse monastic ideals into his missionary activity, establishing a monastic settlement on Spruce Island, Alaska. The Aleuts were too childlike to be able to quickly become the bearers of the monastic inheritance, and the white men were too busy with worldly pursuits. Nevertheless, St. Herman made at least one naval officer, Simeon Yanovsky (see *The Orthodox Word*, Vol. 26, nos. 1-2, pp. 4-109), his spiritual son. Later, back in Russia, Elder Anthony directed Yanovsky's soul in such a way that he became a Schemamonk with the new name Sergius. Schemamonk Sergius died in the Kaluga Monastery: the same monastery whence would later come the founder of the St. Herman of Alaska Brotherhood, Archimandrite Gerasim. Fr. Gerasim re-founded the original monastery of St. Herman on Spruce Island (New Valaam), where in 1963 our St. Herman Brotherhood was born.

St. Herman had predicted that thirty years after his repose people would remember him. And so it happened that Schemamonk Sergius, having first received Orthodoxy in America, provided Valaam Monastery with the basic hagiographical information about St. Herman, which was published thirty years after the Saint's repose. He compiled this information while living under the spiritual direction of Optina Elder Anthony. The Life of St. Herman was published by Valaam at about the same time that the Life of St. Anthony was published by Optina. Thus, in a mystical way, Elder Anthony inspired our Brotherhood to publish material on St. Herman and other spiritual texts, which eventually resulted in the volume which the reader is now holding. A good portion of this volume contains writings of Schemamonk Sergius Yanovsky describing the spiritual inheritance which he received from Fr. Anthony.

II

The story of how this bibliographic rarity was reprinted a little over one hundred years after its initial publication is described below so as to show the contemporary reader how, in the spiritual life, the will of people on earth and the will of the saints in heaven are intertwined. We believe that the publication of this *Optina Series* is a direct result of the efforts of the genuine lovers of Optina Monastery, who cared for that refined citadel of spirituality and willed both the existence of our Brotherhood and the revival of Optina Monastery in Russia.

As a note of interest we add that Elder Anthony has been glorified as a Saint in no other place than here in America. In Russia he still has not been canonized.

Through the good fortune of God's Providence, the editors of the St. Herman Brotherhood have, from its very inception, been in immediate contact with people who were spiritual children and carriers of the fervency and traditions of the great Optina Monastery. My personal conversion took place through spiritual children of the last Optina Elder, St. Nectarius. It was Fr. Vladimir who cared to convert me to the Truth, and directed me to his elder, Fr. Adrian, who literally *lived* on the teachings of St. Nectarius, having been his spiritual son in Russia. My formation was zealously guarded by Fr. Adrian, who kept careful watch that I would not go astray and take for granted the gift of Orthodoxy, as is so often the case amidst Orthodox Russians of today. The bishop who ordained us, Bishop Nektary, was another disciple of St. Nectarius; he was often concerned that our Brotherhood might slip into taking Church life for granted, without appreciating that which had been handed down to us. The publishing activity of our Brotherhood was constantly scrutinized by other disciples of Optina traditions, who set us upon the missionary path of the printed word in the Optina tradition. Professor I. M. Kontzevitch (the brother of Bishop Nektary) and his wife Helen kept abreast of our progress to the very day of their deaths. Even the man who blessed the Brotherhood of

St. Herman of Alaska—the desert-dweller Fr. Gerasim of Spruce Island—came from the Optina territory and used to have Elder Joseph of Optina as his confessor—his own elder, Ioasaph, being a disciple of Elder Macarius of Optina.

The first Russian-language book that our Brotherhood published was an Optina journal, *On the Banks of God's River: Vol. II.* Also, the first, most complete book on Optina Monastery published to date, the 600-page volume *Optina Monastery and Its Era*, was written by I. M. and Helen Kontzevitch with our extensive participation. In 1965, when the St. Herman of Alaska Brotherhood's magazine, *The Orthodox Word*, began to come out, thousands of copies of this "strong Orthodox food" began to reach all the corners of the English-speaking world and the movement of Orthodox converts began to rely on it. At this time my partner, Fr. Seraphim, began to be concerned that in Russia—from where Orthodoxy had come to America in the first place—people were sitting in prisons, facing the ruins of once-glorious Optina, and were not even receiving the crumbs from our American tables. Thirty years ago it was unthinkable to even dream of the death of Communism and the revival of Optina Monastery. Thirty years ago, when American converts began to grow and flourish on Optina's "nourishing victuals," poor Russian youths were growing up without the slightest idea that from within their bosom there had come forth such inspiring, potent literature, which could turn some "American Okies" into traditional carriers of Optina Spirituality. And why not? American freedom is capable of raising whole citadels of followers of Christ, once the genuine impetus is placed on fertile American soil.

III

One day in our forlorn northern wilderness, we had just finished Matins and the monastic meal in the refectory, during which some account from Optina had been read. Fr. Seraphim, after sitting with a grave face and listening intently to the reading and my comments on how it is impossible to translate a particular term known in Patristic language as *smirennomudriye* (wisdom derived from humility), looked up with a question: "Who would best personify that virtue?" I saw in him a spark of inspiration which, from past experience, I knew to be charged with creative energy. He was wondering which spiritual elder to write about for publication; and I, knowing that my answer to his question would "jump-start" his soul's activity, lamented, "Oh, what's the use?! The spiritual image of such men is too boring and too bland for our American psychology. It does not have enough weight to sink into the soul of modern man, who has been raised solely on superficiality and takes life as a game." And I sunk into silence.

Among our brothers—who were all very young, naive, and definitely still external in accepting the Orthodox, traditional way of life—some were seriously eager to try out the monastic path. They were no different from all the "average Joes" of today. Fr. Seraphim lifted his eyes on them with a feeling of compassion and whispered to me an urgent demand: "Who?! Who personifies that virtue?" "Elder Anthony of Optina," I quietly retorted, but then added, "Oh, what's the use?!"

That was enough for Fr. Seraphim. He rang the bell to rise for the thanksgiving prayer, after which he said: "You are right. We need him, here as well as in Russia. Let's give him back to Russia, and then we will have him here." He resolved to have his life in print, both in Russian and in English.

IV

Elder Anthony (Putilov) of Optina was the younger brother of Moses, the Abbot of Optina, who was responsible for founding the famous Optina Skete and gathering the successors of the disciples of St. Paisius Velichkovsky. Abbot Moses also gathered the writings and translations of St. Paisius, which were circulated almost on an "underground" level in manuscripts carefully copied in calligraphic style and treasured by true lovers of monasticism at the turn of the 19th century.

The Putilov brothers, Moses and Anthony, began their monastic life in Sarov, even being instructed by St. Seraphim, and then secluded themselves in a remote gorge in the Roslavl forests, where several hermits lived and preserved the fervency of St. Paisius. This was the cradle out of which arose Optina Monastery as a disseminator of the Paisian inheritance, then in Russia and now in America.

V

I knew nothing of this Optina literary tradition until I received an old book as a gift from my spiritual preceptor, Fr. Vladimir, the faithful disciple of Fr. Adrian. This 424-page book consisted of the letters of Elder Anthony of Optina. Later it became apparent that the reason he had given me this book was that he dearly loved this Elder and wanted to introduce me to a different way of seeing spiritual life, which involved man's attuning himself to the will of God. This aspect of spiritual life is absent in today's society. By introducing me to it, Fr. Vladimir gave me an inestimable gift which became a key to the rest of my life. (It is interesting to note that the first person to introduce me to Elder Anthony, Fr. Vladimir, later died on the anniversary of Elder Anthony's death in 1988, and thus is forever united with him in the minds of lovers of Optina.)

At first I found this book of the letters of Elder Anthony to be monotonous, boring reading because it constantly emphasized the humble acceptance of the Providence of God. The advice sounded weak and impotent. Within my heart the world was then still raging—the world with its options and choices, demanding man's will to change the society. I wanted action on my seminary level, but instead, out of the pages of these pastoral counsels came something quiet and meek, as if written in a whisper. Only a few years later—when I was in contact with my dear Professor and Mrs. Kontzevitch, and had actually read the full biography of Elder Anthony compiled by his closest disciples—did it begin to dawn on me that there was another logic that had escaped me earlier simply because I had been "too loud."

When I borrowed the biography of Elder Anthony from the Kontzeviches, I held it with trepidation. This book was from the very library of the Optina Skete and had been miraculously discovered by Helen Kontzevitch in the hands of a Paris book peddler who had received it from Russia as "junk" after the famous monastery had been closed. Mrs. Kontzevitch sold her belongings in order to get money by which to rescue this book and others from the destroyed Optina Monastery. As I sat in a bus reading the old pages which even "smelled" of Holy Russia, I realized that that very volume had been read by Optina monks, including the Elders Ambrose, Hilarion, Anatole, Barsanuphius, Joseph and my beloved Nectarius, who seemed to smile, peeping right out of the book. The image I encountered from this volume was that of a humble, desert-dwelling youth who was even granted to behold Divine Uncreated Light. The image from the biography hinted to my soul of something which might be called "the energy of transmission," a sort of initiation into a lifestyle wherein a patristic code of values prevailed. Having read the book, I could not part with it and carried it with me for months. I longed for the world of that loving, whispering state of caring and guarding one's soul as something precious. I know that when one is in that state, whenever God so wills He is able to touch the soul with a "smile," and this is followed by *umileniye* or tenderness of heart. I wanted that world. I was given the means—I had my Optina instructors. Now I had the tools, the books, even from the very library of Optina Skete which these holy men and Elder Anthony had erected.

The Soviets have now deprived us of the buildings, the woods, and even the land of Optina. Their satanic hatred attempted to erase those humble, holy abodes from the face of the earth. They demolished the graves of the holy Elders at Optina, pouring cold, gray cement over them, and then made a garage for repairing trucks over the hallowed ground wherein lay great saints and Church Fathers of universal significance. They attempted to kill the soul of the carriers of Holy Russia. They fooled the whole world through propaganda, even ecclesiastical propaganda, so as to silence that inner silence which nothing can muffle. Yet I heard that silence and it resounded throughout my whole being. That night, carrying the book and wandering in the woods of Monterey, I made the resolve: I would amplify that "sound of silence"—Elder Anthony's humility. When I met the young, future Father Seraphim and took him to those woods in order to read to him portions of Elder Anthony's life, he, too, was deeply inspired and waited for the God-ordained time when we would have our American desert and could make the image of the meek Anthony heard loud and clear. Eventually, I inherited the book together with others, some even from the same library of Optina Skete.

VI

Now the time was ripe: we had our monastery in the woods, we had the books. We had the eager, youthful listeners. They were perhaps not ready, but Fr. Seraphim was. He made a resolve to get Russian-language type and print these books for Russia, one by one, smuggling them through the prism of Soviet godlessness into the very geographical spot where Optina lay.

We knew that on this spot (Optina) there was a "Dostoevsky Museum," and we considered that it had to have a library to which we could send such books, having multiplied in American freedom the Optina inheritance. And it worked.

One of the young men who was with us at the time—being naive and fresh as a daisy, having caught the fervency of our inspiration—watched carefully the outcome of the after-refectory conversation. He pondered these thoughts in his heart and, in a short while, announced his decision to give up everything and go to a monastery. He had $900 in his bank account. Following the monastic tradition he wanted to give his money to the poor. Now he knew that "the poor" are the Russians who were in a land enslaved by militant atheists and who would, once Communism cracked, be able to hear about the Elders. Thus, he gave the money for this cause, and soon our first book in the Optina series was published and sent to Russia. This was the life of Elder Anthony. Only after the fall of the godless regime did we find out that our Optina books had indeed found their way to Optina and had been the initial inspiration for the young monks to restore that monastery. When we had the fortune of making a pilgrimage to Optina in 1991 and visit the heart of Optina Skete—the cell of Elder Ambrose, wherein all the Optina Elders generated their teaching and formed young souls—we were surprised to learn that there was, among others, a portrait of our Fr. Seraphim in that cell. The Abbot of Optina invited us for dinner and, after greeting us with a sermon, presented us with an icon of Elder Nectarius, saying that it was a gift of gratitude to us for taking part in the restoration of the broken heart of Optina Monastery through our publications.

THIS BOOK was originally intended as a tool whereby we can see a man struggling for his soul's salvation, without any

The cell or "khibarka" of Elder Ambrose in the Skete as it looks today, where a picture of Fr. Seraphim Rose is placed among other portraits. It is preserved so as to look just like it did during the time of Elders Ambrose, Joseph and Nectarius.

layers of psychological, emotional or theological veneer. We find these layers in most of today's biographies, which are written with the aim of "discovering" inward psychological motives and reading into the life of a man ideas and realities which are actually just modern fashions and were not present in former centuries, when life was more simple. This is especially evident in biographies which deal with people of past centuries, far removed from our times.

When this book was first printed by us in Russian in 1973, we addressed it to the young generation of Russians, languishing in the atheistic wasteland which was once Holy Russia. We were hoping to awaken them to the wealth of Optina spirituality. Now—two decades later—Russia is free and Optina is alive. But the dark clouds of militant atheism are hovering over our freedom-loving Americans, who, having gone through cycles of search for Truth, be it a genuine search for God or just the following of fashion, are now discovering spirituality in Holy Russia. At this late hour may they be aroused to do God's work. As then for the Russian edition, so now for the first American edition we write:

The time has come! The spiritual fields have long since been ripe for the harvest and it is time for the workers to step forward. May this image of the Elder wondrous in Divine meekness, Abbot Anthony, help them! May young American souls be inspired by the spiritual world of Elder Anthony! May they be strengthened by the meekness and patience which led Fr. Anthony to heaven!

May those who are ready to give their life for the love of Christ burn with zeal according to God! America awaits them.

Holy Father Anthony, pray to God for us!

Abbot Herman
St. Herman of Alaska Monastery
Mid-Pentecost, 1994

Elder Anthony
† 1865

FOREWORD
to the Russian Edition

At the end of the present age will the saints be as numerous throughout the world as they are now?" a certain one asked St. Niphon of Constantia. The Blessed Elder replied, "My son, unto the very end of this age prophets of the Lord God will not fail, nor will the ministers of Satan. However," he added, "in the last times those who will truly serve God will succeed in hiding themselves from men."

The truth of these words has come to pass in our time. Amidst the general decline of faith and piety, visible and evident to all, there have been in our time many great hierarchs and worthy priests, renowned for both their gift of preaching and their lofty way of life, and many hermits and monks zealous of treading the path of the ancient holy fathers. It is worthy of our attention that such great ascetics of piety in the 19th century in Russia are not fewer than in other ages more conducive to monasticism. We do not even know if there ever lived in our fatherland almost simultaneously such beacons of monasticism as in our days: Seraphim of Sarov and the other ascetics of Sarov, Nazarius of Valaam, Elder Theodore of Sanaxar, George of Zadonsk, Basil Kishkin, Peter Michurin, Zosima Verkhovsky and Basilisk, Schemamonks Theodore and Cleopas, Macarius of Pesnosha, Hilarion of Troekurovo, Theophan of New Lake,

John of Sezenovo, Daniel of Siberia, Parthenius of Kiev, Amphilochius and Innocent of Rostov, Alexander of Arzamas, Theodore of Novospassky, Leonid, Macarius and Moses of Optina, Timon Nadeyevsky, Amphilochius of Rekon, Macarius of the Altai, Philaret of Glinsk, Anikita Shirinsky-Shakhmatov. Likewise, the ascetics of the more or less well-known hermitages of White Bluff, Ploshchansk, St. Nicephorus and others, and these entire host of holy fathers of our time whom Orthodox Russia knows well, but about whom one part of our society knows almost nothing, and whose life serves as a heavy reproach to many of us. To the ranks of these people, who have demonstrated by their life that true monasticism is possible in our times, belongs the brother of the later Fr. Moses the Archimandrite of Optina, Abbot Anthony, whose biography is now presented to the reader.

Information about him has been taken from the following sources:

First, from his own personal notes, and from his letters to various people, especially to his older brother, Archimandrite Moses.

Second, from books: a) *A Historical Description of the Skete of Optina Monastery of the Entrance of the Theotokos near Kozelsk*, compiled by Hieromonk (later Archimandrite) Leonid [Kavelin], St. Petersburg, 1862; b) *A Historical Description of the Maloyaroslavets Black Island Monastery of St. Nicholas*, compiled by the same writers, St. Petersburg, 1863; and c) from articles by the same writer, *The Last Russian Orthodox Desert-dwellers*, printed in *Domestic Conversations*, 1862, issues 20-26.

Third, from stories, letters and memoirs of spiritual children of Abbot Anthony and other trustworthy people who knew him. The Letters of Abbot Anthony were published as a separate book in Moscow in 1869.

FOREWORD

If any of the readers know something noteworthy about the life of the reposed Elder which is not in the biography published by us, we humbly ask them to inform us so that we can supplement the biography in a future edition, and also use the new information for our own edification.

September 28th, 1869
Optina Monastery

ОПТИНСКІЙ СТАРЕЦЪ ИГУМЕНЪ АНТОНІЙ

Line engraving of Elder Anthony by Natalia Kareva,
Moscow, 1994. At left, St. Sergius of Radonezh.

THE LIFE OF
ELDER ANTHONY
OF OPTINA

Serpukhov Vysotsky Monastery as it looks today,
with no change since the time of Elder Anthony's youth.

I

Childhood

AND THE FIRST YEARS OF HIS YOUTH

1795-1816

Abbot Anthony—in the world, Alexander Ivanovich Putilov—was born on March 9, 1795, in the town of Romanov in the Yaroslavl Province. His parents, Ivan Grigoryevich and Anna Ivanovna Putilov, were native residents of the town of Serpukhov, but later became registered as Moscow merchants. They were pious and God-fearing people and raised their children in the fear of God, in the spirit of strict Orthodoxy, teaching them from an early age to love the Church of God with its holy services.* As a child, young Alexander was very quiet and modest. He did not like the noisy games of his playmates, and in his youth was protected by the fear of God from passions harmful to his soul. Even in his childhood he felt an inclination toward monasticism. Previously some of his relatives had devoted their lives to monasticism; his great-grandfather Joel was a hierodeacon of the Serpukhov Monastery, and his cousin Maximillia was a nun at the Ascension Convent in Moscow, distinguishing herself by her strict ascetic life. In general, throughout the entire Putilov family there was an inclination

---

* See the private notes of Abbot Anthony in Part II, describing his childhood up to the age of fourteen.

toward monasticism. Of Alexander's four brothers only one (Basil) chose family life. Another (Cyril), although he remained a layman, was not married and was a righteous man. The other two brothers, Timothy and Jonah, like Alexander, left the world in their youth, and it is especially notable that all three of them later became commendable abbots in well-known Russian monasteries. Their elder sister Anysia also wanted to enter a convent, but against her own will she had to marry. After three years she died, while still in the flower of her youth; and her husband, as if fulfilling his wife's desire, became a monk.

Alexander was ten years old when his older brothers Timothy and Jonah left the world and entered Sarov Monastery. It is likely that their example influenced their younger brother, with whom they corresponded, occasionally sending edifying books as well.

Alexander, at that time thirteen years old, wrote, among other things, to his brothers in Sarov: "One of the books you sent me greatly impressed me, and I want to follow a rule from it, which is: *To hold the world in contempt and to seek the Heavenly Kingdom is the highest wisdom. By stillness and silence the pious soul is greatly strengthened and understands the mysteries of the Scripture. Thus, if anyone abandons the world, God and His holy angels will visit him.* I wish and desire to be as you are. Even though I don't yet know what to do, I still desire to be like you."

Alexander, who had such exalted feelings as a child, passed through many severe trials in his childhood, indicating that God was preparing him for some special task. Ten times his life was in great danger. Once he almost drowned, another time he fell down from such a height that he fractured his skull. Each time, however, he was saved from death by God's Providence which guarded him. Also, he was also so often gravely ill that, according to his own words, some centenarians had not had as many illnesses as he had already experienced, being only fifteen years old. During these illnesses he learned patience and was being prepared for the many grave illnesses with which his life would be filled. At the same time, it seemed that those physical sufferings which he had experienced early in his childhood helped to reveal his inclination toward spiritual life. Thus, soon after writing the letter from which we have quoted, Alexander fell very ill and, when he had somewhat recovered, he wrote again to his elder brother:

"During my sickness I read the book that you are familiar with. This book should be regarded as *soul-saving*. It influenced me in such a way that all I now think about is a passport and Sarov Hermitage, that is, to secure my passport and to go to the Sarov Hermitage. I don't know if I will be with *you*, yet I must come. So I humbly ask you, is it possible to send me the passport somehow? If it is possible, let me know by letter, sending it in my name by the first return post." This letter was written in November of 1808.

Yet, obviously the time of God's will for Alexander to leave the world had not yet come, as this letter fell into his parents' hands. On this occasion the thirteen-year-old lover of the ascetic life "suffered rather painfully," as he later expressed. He had to postpone his plan and obey the will of his father, who had also not allowed his eldest sons to enter the monastery quickly nor without difficulty.

In 1809 their father died. Alexander, who was making arrangements for the funeral, found consolation in dressing the deceased all in black like a monk. His mind was constantly occupied solely by the thought of going to the monastery. After paying his last respects to his father, Alexander with his older brother Cyril, in whose care he had been left by his dying father and who was also his godfather, went from Mologa, where the Putilov father had been living at that time, to Moscow. Alexander was given a position working for the merchant Karpishev, for whom his elder brothers had worked previously. In his spare time Alexander loved to visit churches and monasteries. In this way, having lived in Moscow only three years, he knew the holy places of Moscow better than many long-time residents. Even in his old age he remembered where certain churches were located and where the wonder-working icons were.

In 1812, at the time of the Napoleonic invasion, Alexander had to undergo another trial. When the French were approaching Moscow, his landlord, among the first to flee from Moscow, left him with his brother Cyril to guard the house. After hiding all the valuables with the help of some seemingly good people (who later were the first to reveal to the French the place where they had hidden them), they also thought about escaping from the approaching enemies, but it was already too late.

While they were leaving Moscow—this was the 2nd of September at three o'clock in the afternoon—a Pole on horseback rode up to Alexander and, placing the barrel of a pistol to his head, said: "Your money!" Alexander, in order to save his life, surrendered his purse with his gold. Later, the enemy soldiers robbed Alexander of his watch and clothes and drove him along half-naked. Alexander spent ten days as a prisoner of the French, was an eyewitness of terrible events, and also suffered much himself. The enemies forced the Russian prisoners to move from place to place heavy loads of things stolen from stores and private homes; they used the Russians as pack animals. Alexander also took part in this wearisome task. He later said, "They loaded us with heavy burdens and beat us, saying, 'Carry them!' And the villains practiced this on my back, too." The Russian prisoners did not have bread and had to eat rotten fish. They ate it while holding their noses, or else they would not have been able to swallow it. The prisoners had it so bad in Moscow that it was thought that even in hell they would have been better off. In relating this, Fr. Anthony added, "St. John

Panorama of the Moscow Kremlin in the 19th century.
(A postcard from the 19th century.)

Chrysostom writes that the very worst sufferings on earth are child's play in comparison with the least sufferings in hell. But we talked this way at the time because we knew no better way to express the anguish of a French prison." In those days, the ringing of bells was not heard in Moscow. This weighed even more on the heart of Alexander, who was accustomed to daily services in all the churches. So if someone, Frenchman or Russian, ever accidently struck a bell, this sorrowful sound brought consolation to his soul.

It did not occur to the prisoners to try to escape because the French had spread rumors that St. Petersburg and other cities had fallen into their hands. Finally, finding out from someone that those rumors were false and that there were Russian soldiers not far from Moscow, Alexander decided to escape. At midnight on the 12th of September, while it was raining heavily, he managed to get away from his torturers with the help of a peasant, the slave-of-God Thomas. Hiding under a small bridge, he escaped from the persecution of his enemies and from further tortures. However, after having been robbed he had to spend the night in a field, barefoot and half-naked. He would have gravely suffered the consequences of the cold and damp if he had not come across, by the mercy of God, a group of his fellow countrymen who like him were hiding from the enemies. He even found among them some of his relatives, who with joy received the young sufferer and sheltered him from the severe weather. They walked at night through forests, swamps, and ravines; and during the day they hid in the forests in order to avoid meeting the enemy. Finally, they reached the road to Ryazan. Later, Alexander liked to recall all that he endured at that time and how he was saved from further danger, perceiving in it the action of God's Providence.

Succeeding, with the help of God and not without difficulty, in escaping from Moscow, he arrived at his relatives' in

Rostov wearing plain sandals and having lost everything he had earned in Moscow. Time passed and the enemy was chased out of Russia. Even then, so many obstacles presented themselves that he was still unable to separate himself from the world. After waiting for a while and receiving no information about his older brother Timothy, Alexander, in order to avoid idleness, finally decided to take a job with a Mr. Priklonsky, similar to the one he had had in Moscow. In his thoughts, however, he still aspired to the spiritual life and with great zeal visited churches and monasteries. He especially liked to visit the St. James Monastery in Rostov, where he would help the Elder, Fr. Amphilochius, to lift the extremely heavy cover from the reliquary of St. Demetrius of Rostov, which was made of the finest Siberian silver and had been donated by the Empress Elizabeth Petrovna.

Alexander avoided the noisy pleasures of the world and preserved himself with such care that, if upon leaving home he would see a woman, he would walk on a different street to avoid meeting her. In spite of the objections of his relatives, he dressed not only modestly but in a very simple manner, not in accord with his status, even wearing a common overcoat. While visiting villages and the countryside as an agent for his merchant, wherever he went he looked for pious and devout old women and, gathering them, conversed with them about spiritual matters. A woman recently died who still remembered the instructive talks of the twenty-year-old man in which his future mission was unwillingly revealed. Having learned from previous experience, he did not tell any of his relatives about his cherished desire except his brother Timothy, and even that he did very cautiously.

At the end of 1815, Alexander decided to leave the world, the circumstances being favorable. First he, like a young elder, secured the future of his older brother, Basil; that is, he chose for him a well-mannered and pious bride. After his brother was

Reliquary of St. Demetrius of Rostov in the St. James Monastery,
where the young Anthony Putilov often went to pray.

married, his relatives tried to talk Alexander into arranging his own life in the same way. He replied that he also found it necessary to change his life, but before doing so he would like to make a trip to Moscow where his elderly mother was living at the time.

Having bought a horse, under the pretext of training it, in the evenings he would visit all the monasteries in Rostov. Stopping at their gates, he would fervently pray to God, the Most Holy Mother of God, and the saints for the successful outcome of his plans. Finally, after obtaining a passport and finding a reliable companion for his trip, Alexander went to Moscow on the 4th of January, 1816. He stopped in a distant suburb of the city (in Taganka) in order to avoid meeting his relatives. Again, he only visited the churches and monasteries in the evening and prayed fervently to God at each entrance. From Moscow he went to Kaluga, unnoticed by anyone, and, after having a *moleben* of thanksgiving to God served there for his safe withdrawal from the bonds of the world, he headed towards the Roslavl Forest where his elder brother had been living as an ascetic for about five years. After bidding farewell to his companion at the village closest to the place where the hermits were living, Alexander rode alone into the thick forest. Not knowing the forest roads, after praying to God he gave his horse free rein, and the horse brought him to his brother's hermitage.

His companion Joseph Antonovich had to suffer much for his participation in Alexander's escape. When he returned to Rostov and appeared before the relatives of the young fugitive without any letter from him and told them where he had left Alexander, no one believed him. The suspicion arose that he had killed Alexander. Poor Joseph was put into prison and spent half a year there, until a letter arrived from Timothy confirming that Alexander was really staying with him.

The Optina Skete forest, which separates the Monastery from the world. The path, which connects the Monastery with the Skete, was often trodden by the Putilov brothers.

2

Life in the Roslavl Forests

1816-1821

IN EARLIER TIMES in the Roslavl Forest of the Smolensk Province, there lived a family of silence-loving hermits who were honored as Elders: Barnabas, Nicetus, James, Basilisk, Zosima, Adrian, Athanasius and others. The place where the Roslavl ascetics lived belonged to the landowner Damian Mikhailovich Bronevsky, who had his summer cottages on an estate three miles away from the village of Yakima, at a distance of about twenty-seven miles from the city of Roslavl. At that time all the desert-dwellers were living in three cells. Hiero-schemamonk Athanasius lived in a cell about a thousand yards away from Fr. Dositheus, and about the same distance away from Fr. Dorotheus.

In 1811, Alexander's older brother Timothy (Moses) became a member of this family. Alexander wanted to devote himself to the monastic life and came to see his brother in order to ask his advice about this, as he had the intention of entering Sarov Monastery. After some discussion with his brother, he decided to stay with him until spring. On January 15, 1816, they clothed him as a novice. To the twenty-year-old Alexander, who had striven so long and so zealously toward monastic life, the short, dyed *podrasnik*, covered with stains and patches, seemed, as he himself later expressed it, "more precious than royal purple."

In the spring Fr. Moses told him, "He who does not sow now will reap nothing." Alexander prolonged his stay. Together they planted vegetables, harvested them in the fall, and then went on a pilgrimage to Kiev. On their return they visited the Sophroniev, Glinsk, and Ploschansk Hermitages, where they saw and conversed with many elders of exalted spiritual life. On this trip Alexander visited all these monasteries, but his heart was not inclined to any one of them. After they returned from Kiev to their place of solitude, Alexander continued his visit, not wishing to leave. "And in this way, coming only for a visit, I stayed with my brother for twenty-four years," Alexander often related later.

From his early youth, Alexander with great zeal dedicated himself to the labors of desert-dwelling. Having possessed great physical strength from his childhood, despite the illnesses he frequently suffered from, he did not spare himself from this time onward. He performed great ascetic labors which to many in our weak times would seem unbelievable. Arising at midnight, he and his brother would, by themselves and without the slightest omission, read through the entire order of the cycle of services. Alexander, having constantly and zealously gone to God's Church as a child, knew well the complete order of the services and had a special inclination and ability to learn the church typicon. Through daily immersion in church services over many years, he perfected his knowledge of them and acquired such excellent skill that it was hard to find anyone who could compare with him.

He also labored in copying by hand the patristic books in the traditional way, and helped his brother in compiling several collections of manuscripts which contained a systematic order of the rules for Christians, especially for the monastic life. These extraordinary collections prove with what care and understanding both brothers read the works of the Spirit-bearing Fathers. Unto ripe old age they liked reading spiritual and other generally useful books, and therefore they not only had an extensive knowledge of spiritual matters, but were also knowledgeable in many other fields. It is also remarkable that Alexander, like his older brother, out of great reverence for the patristic books, always read and wrote in a standing position, even after having stood a long time chanting the services. He often spent eighteen out of twenty-four hours standing on his feet, and in several years did such damage to his legs that it later developed into pain from which he suffered until his death.

Besides these ascetic labors, Alexander, as the junior member of the family of recluses, with zeal and great fervency performed many other difficult tasks of obedience. It was his duty to awaken the others; therefore, without fail he had to arise before everyone else in order to start reading his own prayers at the proper time. He also had to cut firewood in the surrounding forest and carry it to the cells. He was in charge of the vegetable garden, where he could grow only turnips because of the infertility of the soil. There, too, he usually had to work when he was already tired after having read the daily prayer-rule, and could expect afterwards only a frugal meal which he prepared by himself. After doing such tasks, in addition to the common prayers, each one of them had to read his own cell-rule, accompanied by prostrations. All this was done with great diligence, living on extremely meager lenten food, which barely satisfied their hunger and did not strengthen their bodies. They permitted themselves to eat fish only on great feasts, and even oil seldom appeared in their meals; but in their hard life even dry bread seemed to them sweet and tasty, as Fr. Anthony would say. They ate it with great gratitude to God as His gift to them, and with great care, as if eating *antidoron*. Anything else sent to them in addition to the dry bread they received as a great mercy from the Lord and ascribed it with sincere faith to the special Providence of God. Once, a farmer passing by on his way to the forest left the hermits a bag of peas. The hermits received that little donation with gratitude to God, as if it had come directly from His hands. People who have always lived in prosperity and have never experienced deprivation would not understand this.

On great feasts all the elders gathered in the cell of Fr. Athanasius for the common service. After the service they ate together and sometimes strengthened themselves by drinking tea (or, for the lack of tea, some other herb), since they were exhausted by their years of many labors; but the new novice Alexander in the beginning was refused even that. Later, only after the elders had been treated to it, he was sometimes allowed to drink what was left of it, being very weak tea. It was little more than hot water, yet he drank it, as he later said, with greater pleasure than other people drink fine liqueur. After that the elders would separate until the next feast. At both Pascha and Nativity and on some of the other great feasts as well, the old priest from the nearest village, Lugi (about five miles away), came and gave the hermits the reserved Holy Gifts.

Neither beasts nor people disturbed the peace of soul of the Roslavl hesychasts. During the entire winter, wolves would howl around their cells, but the elders were used to their howling as if it were the wailing of the wind. Bears sometimes plundered their vegetable gardens but never touched the hermits. Only once did such a temptation come close to them. The sheriff of Roslavl, hearing that "rich Moscow merchants" (as Fr. Moses and his brother were called) lived in the forest, decided to visit them in order to inspect their papers and make sure that they were not Old Believers.* But God spared His servants from this temptation. The whole day the sheriff rode around their cells but could not find them, although he came close to approaching them from several different directions.

It is known from experience that the beginning of the monastic life is very important, and success in this endeavor very much depends upon how strong in the very beginning is the desire to become an ascetic. After he had chosen his brother for his elder and spiritual director, Alexander committed himself to obedience to him with complete faith and burning determination, which also showed in his ascetic labors. At the same time, this obedience made his difficult life easier to bear. Here is how Fr. Anthony later wrote to one of his disciples for his edification concerning his entry into the monastic life:

"When I felt that in my heart the flames of love for God had begun to burn, all earthly cares appeared to me loathsome and prosperity repellent; and I ran away from Rostov like a bird from a net or a thirsty deer and settled in an impassable wilderness, hoping that God would deliver me from faintheartedness and from the many sins which possessed me. I wholly surrendered myself to unremitting obedience to my Elder, Fr. Moses, and, thanks to the Lord God, I have never regretted once having done so."

Alexander sincerely loved his older brother and elder as a father, yet at the same time feared him as the Superior. In his presence he always remained absolutely silent, and this silence made him a lover of wisdom and helped him to acquire great spiritual discretion. Once while he was still a novice, at a meeting

---

* Schismatic Orthodox believers who refused to accept the reforms of Patriarch Nikon in the seventeenth century.

of elders who were discussing a subject known to him, in listening to them he became carried away and spoke several words. He collected himself immediately and, feeling ashamed of his audacity, blushed and became silent. See how strict and attentive he was to himself! He also fled conversations with strangers. As he related afterwards, from his entrance into the monastic life over the course of fourteen years, that is, until the time he left the Roslavl forests and had already lived in the Optina Skete, he never allowed himself to engage in conversation with strangers visiting the Monastery. "And when someone asked me where a certain cell was," Alexander said, "I used to point at it with my finger and keep silent."

While avoiding unnecessary contact with people at the very beginning of his monastic life, he did not lose love for his neighbor. "While living in the Roslavl Forest," Fr. Anthony said later about himself, "if I happened to meet a man, I felt as happy as if he were an angel of God; but now, no matter how glad I feel, it's no longer the same. It's gone!" the Elder repeated and then sighed.

In general, in his later years when he had attained great spiritual heights, Fr. Anthony loved to reminisce with special joy about his desert-dwelling life in the Roslavl Forest. Then his face would become especially radiant and full of inspiration.

Labor, effort, struggles, and temptations could not be avoided when undertaking such an exalted life. Even in his old age Fr. Anthony remembered vividly how, when he was a novice, his elders would send him to the vegetable garden during their rest, and how he would sometimes feel exhausted physically and mentally.

His Elder Fr. Moses treated him quite severely. If Alexander overslept and was late in waking others for the midnight service, he was given prostrations for being slothful, and if he did something else wrong, prostrations again. In the beginning he

Elder Moses Putilov
†1862

fulfilled these penances with great effort and hardship, but afterwards he became so accustomed to them that he sometimes missed them if for a long time he had not heard the familiar words, "Well, brother, start the prostrations!" His patience and obedience were tested many times. "In the beginning of my sojourn in the wilderness," as he later related about himself, "I had a most unendurable character, and my Elder had to try different approaches in order to subdue my obstinacy. But nothing could humble my rebelliousness more than cleaning the latrines several times annually over a period of six years. In addition, I was often sent on the roads for horse and cattle manure for the fertilization of the vegetable gardens. Initially I performed this holy obedience not without sorrow and tears."

"Performing these tasks of obedience," he said on another occasion, "I remembered once my former life and my mind started to waver. I thought, 'People my age are counting their earnings, and I have to occupy myself with this!' Soon I realized that I was wrong and started to feel sorry that I had dared to grumble at my Elder in my thoughts, and feeling ashamed I confessed my thoughts to him. After a lecture of which I was very deserving, I received forgiveness and treasured it as if it came from the Lord Himself, and with great joy continued to force myself to be patient in performing ascetic labors." "…Without humbling oneself in spirit one cannot be saved. Humility cannot be learned from mere words; it is necessary to practice it, and someone has to hammer us flat. Without humility it is hard to enter into the Kingdom of God, which is obtained through many sorrows."

The difficulties of the narrow and sorrowful path of the monastic life became joyful to Alexander through rewards of spiritual consolations full of grace. Once on a dark autumn night, Fr. Moses awakened the young ascetic: "Get up, brother, we need to see if perhaps there might not be some fish in the nets." The river was not close at all. With the words, "Bless, Batiushka," the humble novice arose and went into the thick forest. The rainy autumn midnight, the murmur of the forest, the hoots of the owls—all of this disturbed and initially scared him, but obedience prevailed; he took heart and made an effort to go ahead, hoping that the prayers of the Elder would protect him from any evil. With prayer on his lips, he groped along almost by memory and came to his destination. Of course, he did not find anything in the nets and returned back towards his cell. Now instead of fear, he felt in his heart a great joy, and suddenly it became lighter and lighter in front of him, as if the dark night had turned into a bright day. After a short time, it became dark again; but the heart of Alexander was filled with an ineffable joy seldom experienced on earth, and then by only a few people. In spiritual ecstasy he returned to the Elder, told him about his vision, and was unable to fall asleep the whole night; it seemed to him that he was in Paradise—so much did his soul rejoice!

Another time, at Holy Pascha, after the radiant service of Matins and the Hours had been sung, he was sent to walk alone in the forest, and in the silent forest on that exalted day he experienced such delightful consolation and spiritual ecstasy, as if he were in heaven and not on earth. Thus Alexander, in forcing himself to achieve complete obedience and to cut off his own will, felt in his soul ineffable delight and peace. But it was not at once and not without effort that he obtained that blessed sorrowlessness and peace of soul.

In the first year of his monastic life he had moments of severe melancholy, and many times in his thoughts he was about to leave. "But," as he later related, "I was restrained from doing so by the words of Christ: *No man having put his hand to the plough and looking back is fit for the Kingdom of God* (Luke 9:62). Since I did not wish to perish, I decided it is better to suffer with the people of God than to live in the dwellings of sinners (cf. Heb. 11:25) and to comfort myself by all sorts of earthly pleasures."

Once this depression became so strong and the ascetic life appeared to him so hard and unbearable, that he took his knapsack and decided to run away; but after walking a short distance he returned and set to his obedience again. Emerging victoriously from these and similar temptations and persevering in such a severe and strict life, Alexander prepared himself for the hardships which further awaited him in the monastic life. After his experiences in the beginning, monastic life began to appear easier and more bearable. At the same time, he was later able to feel great compassion for his weaker brothers due to his own experience with human weakness.

In 1819, the great ascetic Fr. Theophan died in Alexander's arms. Fr. Theophan had been a monk of Optina Monastery and had at times visited the desert-dwellers for the benefit of his soul. Once he had spent forty days without any food, performing great ascetic labors. Alexander had forgotten to ask Fr. Theophan to pray for him before the latter reposed; on the fortieth day Fr. Theophan appeared to him in a dream. Alexander said to him, "Father, I was going to ask you to pray for me before the throne of God, but I didn't." Fr. Theophan replied, "I pray for you to God just the same. Basil the Great says, 'He who prays for others, prays for himself.'" Fr. Anthony said that this Elder, while still alive, had such a radiant, grace-filled countenance that one did not dare to look him straight in the eyes, but could only glance at him from the side.

After four years in the novitiate, Alexander was clothed in the angelic schema on February 2nd, 1820, the Feast of the Meeting of the Lord, and was given the name Anthony. The tonsure was performed in his cell by Hiero-schemamonk Athanasius, and his Elder "from the mantle" was his older brother, Fr. Moses. In later years, Fr. Anthony remembered with

The Optina Monastery Catholicon, dedicated to the Entry of the
Theotokos into the Temple, as it looked then and looks now,
after its restoration.

delight how joyful was his first monastic nameday on the 17th of January [the Feast of St. Anthony the Great], in 1821. He spent this day in silence and prayer in the midst of the impassable wilderness, keeping vigil all night. "Truly," he said, "I felt then the Pascha of the Lord within my soul." Some of Fr. Anthony's spiritual children asked him how long he was able to preserve in his heart the special action of grace felt by many people who are tonsured. Fr. Anthony revealed that he was in this state for a whole year.

After a stay of five years in the Roslavl Forest, Alexander's destiny took him to the place where, by the will of God, he spent the greater part of his monastic life, that is, to the Kozelsk Optina Monastery in the Kaluga Diocese. This occurred in the following manner:

At that time Bishop Philaret, who later became Metropolitan of Kiev, was head of the diocese. This hierarch, who since his early youth had loved the monastic life with his whole heart, often visited the monasteries of his diocese and paid special attention to the Optina Monastery, which had been renewed at the end of the previous century by Metropolitan Platon. He admired the beauty of the wooded surroundings occupied by the Monastery. How fitting they were for the ascetic life of the emulators of the ancient Holy Fathers! In the heart of that holy man was born the pious thought to lay the foundation for a skete at the Optina Monastery. This was not only in order to provide for those who wished to live in complete silence, but also to strengthen forever the spiritual life in his favorite monastery. In the meantime, since he had already heard rumors about the ascetic life of the Roslavl hermits, his Eminence turned his attention to them and wished to entrust them with the establishment and management of the proposed skete.

At the end of 1820, it happened that Fr. Moses visited Optina Monastery. The abbot, Fr. Daniel, knowing about the good intention of the bishop, introduced Fr. Moses to him. The monk-loving hierarch received him with fatherly kindness and offered him the opportunity to move to his diocese, together with all the brethren, in order to take charge of the construction and arrangement of a skete in any part of the forest which belonged to the Optina Monastery.

Attracted by the benevolence of the Archpastor and the kindness of the Abbot of the Monastery, Fr. Moses accepted their offer with joy. Upon returning to his solitude, he handed Elder Athanasius the letter to him from the hierarch. He explained in detail to his like-minded brethren all the advantages and spiritual benefits which they would have from the possibilities offered by the well-organized Optina Monastery for their life in solitude, under the patronage of such a God-loving archpastor as Bishop Philaret. Fr. Moses' offer was received with joy. At the general meeting it was decided to accept the invitation, regarding this as the call of God, especially since at the same time, by God's allowance, their peaceful solitude had begun to be undermined by claims of the local land authorities.

On the third of June, 1821, Fr. Moses with Fr. Anthony and two other devoted monks, Hilarion and Sabbatius, left the Roslavl Forest, according to the wish of the God-loving archpastor. They journeyed with the blessings of the Elders, Athanasius and Dositheus, who did not go with them. The Elders were postponing their move until after the complete establishment of the proposed skete.

ОПТИНА-ПУСТЫНЬ.

The entrance into the Skete—the path leading to the
Church of St. John the Baptist.

3

Life in the Skete of Optina Hermitage

1821-1839

On the 6th of June, 1821, Fr. Anthony with his brother, Fr. Moses, came from the Roslavl Forest to Optina Monastery. After resting there from the trip, they went to Kaluga in order to appear before Bishop Philaret. They were kindly received by him and were given the blessing for the establishment of a skete at Optina Monastery.

They selected the site for the skete in a thick forest on the eastern part of the property, 400 yards from the Monastery. The hermits first cleared huge pines from the site of the skete. With these trees they built a small cell in which initially all five of them lived together. Then they built a church dedicated to St. John the Forerunner of the Lord, and finally started to build dwellings.

When the skete was first established, Fr. Moses was the abbot. Fr. Anthony diligently helped his brother in this work. They worked together with hired hands cutting century-old pines and digging out their large stumps.

On the 24th of August, 1823, Fr. Anthony was ordained hierodeacon, and in 1825, when Fr. Moses became the superior of the Optina Monastery, Fr. Anthony was placed in charge of the Skete. In 1827 he was ordained hieromonk.* When he became the superior of the Skete, he added labor to labor, diligently helping Fr. Moses to raise and strengthen his spiritual offspring.

Fr. Anthony governed the Skete for fourteen years. During this period of time, the Skete was established not only externally, but spiritually also, and thus it began to flourish. Attracted by the good fame of the wise and meek Superior of Optina, elders wise in the spiritual life and steadfast in ascetic labors came from everywhere to the newly established hesychast skete.

In 1829, the well-known Fr. Leonid with five disciples came from the St. Alexander of Svir Monastery. In 1834, Fr. Moses invited Fr. Macarius, the confessor of the Ploshchansk Monastery. With the help of these Elders, the two brothers, who were already experienced spiritual fathers, strove to introduce into the Optina Skete and Monastery the ancient monastic tradition of eldership, thereby strengthening the foundation of the monastic spirit.

Fr. Anthony not only helped the Elders in caring for the spiritual life of the brotherhood by giving them friendly support, but also set himself as an example of complete obedience and devotion to his Elder. In the entire brotherhood there was no novice as humble as the Skete Superior, who never dared to issue any order without the blessing of his Elder, Fr. Moses. There are many handwritten papers, found among other things in his cell after his repose, which confirm what great respect Fr. Anthony had for his Elder. Here is how the name of his older brother is mentioned in them: "Remember, O Lord, my master, spiritual father and benefactor, reverend founder and hieromonk (in some others: Abbot or Archimandrite) Moses."

---

* In the absence of the diocesan bishop, Fr. Anthony was ordained hieromonk in Orel by Bishop Gabriel.

Besides Elders Leonid and Macarius, who came together with Elder Leonid's disciples, there were many outstanding spiritual men who entered the Optina Skete at that time: the seventy-year-old Hiero-schemamonk John, Abbot Barlaam,* Hieromonk Job, Monks Macarius and Gennadius, and the elderly monk Hilarion who reposed at almost one hundred years of age. Optina Skete presented at that time a marvelous sight: a great assembly of gray-haired honorable elders (about twelve of them) who had been through many and diverse trials, both circumstantial and spiritual, and had come from different places and different callings. They had various gifts and traits and were united in one common zealous yearning for genuine spiritual life. In spite of the many differences in personal characteristics, there reigned among them a wonderful harmony. The humble Superior of the Skete, always friendly and treating everyone with respect, shone among them by his diligent deeds for God and sincere love for the Lord and his neighbors.

The high spiritual caliber of the Superior and brethren reigned over the entire outward order of the Skete, including the Divine services and the behavior of the brethren. All of this should be ascribed to the vigilant care of Fr. Anthony.

The following is a comment made during that time by a visitor who was familiar with the Skete and had known the Superior since his youth: "The sublime order and the reflection of a certain unearthly beauty throughout the entire Skete often touched my youthful heart with a spiritual sweetness, which I remember even now with reverence. I consider those days to be the best time of my life. The simplicity and humility of the brethren, everywhere strict order and cleanliness, the abundance of fragrant flowers, and, in general, a pervasive feeling of the

---

* Formerly the Abbot of Valaam Monastery and a friend of St. Herman of Alaska.

presence of heavenly grace made me involuntarily forget everything existing outside of that Monastery. I visited the skete
church primarily at Liturgy. Having just entered, I would
immediately feel outside of this world and its vicissitudes. With
what touching reverence the services were conducted! This
reverence affected all the people present so strongly that every
rustle and every movement in the church could be heard. The
singing of the choir, in which the Skete Superior Fr. Anthony
often participated,* was quiet and harmonious and at the same
time majestic. The choir sang with such order and attention as
I have never heard since then, although I have often heard
professionally trained singers in the capitals and the most famous singers of Europe. In the skete singing one could perceive
meekness, humility, fear of God, and prayerful reverence, while
secular singing reflects the world with its passions, and this is
already mundane. What can I say about those long-awaited days
when the Skete Superior Fr. Anthony would serve? His every
move, every word and exclamation reflected purity, meekness
and reverence, and at the same time a holy feeling of majesty. I
have never seen anywhere else such church services, although I
have visited many monasteries and churches."

At the time of its spiritual flowering, the newly established
Skete and its first inhabitants had to struggle against many
external difficulties and deprivations, especially in the beginning. Because of the small number of brethren, the Superior
fulfilled many of the brothers' obediences. He often had to
manage without any cell-attendant because the one who was
supposed to serve him had to work also as a cook, baker,

---

* Fr. Anthony had a good ear and a pleasant voice, having sung in church
since childhood. He later related, "When I was seven years old, I once sang
by myself the entire Liturgy up to the reading of the Epistle before the readers
arrived, and for that was given two prosphora by the priest."

gardener, and gate-keeper. In 1832, Fr. Anthony wrote to a relative: "I live in my cell alone like the poorest peasant; I personally have to fetch water and wood. We now have in our Skete five ordained priests, but all of them are elderly and ailing, and therefore I alone have to bear the burden of duties for all of us."

Since the establishment of the skete church, the rule of continuous reading of the Psalter had been introduced. Fr. Anthony, even after he had become the Superior, used to have two shifts a day reading the Psalms, and at the most difficult hours: from 1:00 to 2:00 p.m., while all the brethren were resting, and from 11:00 to 12:00 at night. In this way he used to stand on his feet for up to eighteen hours out of twenty-four.

In addition to this, due to his responsibility as Superior, Fr. Anthony fulfilled the duties of guestmaster, receiving visitors with great kindness, sincere friendliness, and love. At that time, with the blessing of the diocesan bishop, women were allowed to come to the skete church to pray at molebens. The duty of serving molebens for the most part lay on Fr. Anthony, and all the visitors found consolation in his diligent and unhurried serving. It sometimes happened that Fr. Anthony was asked to serve a moleben to St. John the Baptist; and he would zealously add to it, for the benefit of the people, a moleben to the Mother of God with an akathist.

In the first years of the Skete, the Superior lived in a small cell in front of the church where later the sacristan lived. At that time life in the Skete was very strict; work was hard and food was meager. However, the hard work made the coarse food pleasant. Fr. Anthony later recalled, "Sometimes after reading my regular prayers I would take an iron shovel and a rake and go to clean the paths. After cleaning all around the Skete and coming to the trapeza, where plain cabbage soup was served, I ate it with great pleasure." It should be mentioned that each section of the skete fence, along which the paths ran, was 500 feet long. If on the great feasts someone from Kozelsk donated wheat loaves for the refectory meal, these loaves were served to the brethren; if not, even on feast days the brethren were content with black bread. Only the Superior had a samovar, and all the brethren gathered no more than twice a week in his cell for tea.

Fr. Anthony, who served as an example of diligence to everyone and labored hard outdoors, did not forget that, according to the teachings of the Holy Fathers, physical work is really a tool for acquiring virtues only if one performs it with humility and spiritual wisdom.

After the repose of Abbot Anthony, unfortunately, only a few pages were found from his diary, written in 1820 in the Roslavl Forest, and at the end of 1823 and the beginning of 1824 in the Skete of the Optina Monastery. We provide these precious fragments in the second part to this book. They indicate with what strict attention the young ascetic (he was thirty years old at the time) watched the inner movements of his heart and with what spiritual self-control he strove to acquire the virtues of the soul: humility, love for one's neighbor, and so forth. The reading of Holy Scripture and the writings of the Holy Fathers with great zeal and love nourished his soul and greatly contributed to this. Also helpful was the fact that he, from the very beginning of his monastic life, had been following that path with determination and obedience. He persevered in cutting off his own will and reasoning before his spiritual father, to whom he submitted himself with complete faith and toward whom he did not change his attitude even while Superior of the Skete.

Soon, in addition to all his voluntary labors, an involuntary cross of grave illness was placed upon him. We have already mentioned by what illnesses God had tested him in his childhood. Later on, from excessive ascetic labor, he developed many

Elder Leonid
†1841

ailments from which he suffered until his death. Because of continuous standing on his feet while praying, his legs hurt; and after some improvement in his legs, he was afflicted with dizziness. He then contracted glaucoma in his eyes and lost his sight for a period of time. When, by the mercy of God, he was healed of that, the affliction in his legs returned and dropsy developed. In 1833, his various diseases became so painful that Fr. Anthony left his duties in the Skete and went to the closest town, Belev, in order to be treated by his acquaintance, Doctor B. Yet, an even graver illness awaited him in the future.

In 1836, on the day of Holy Pascha (the 29th of March), exactly at midnight when Fr. Anthony was hurrying to Matins on the forest path leading to the Monastery, he hit his right foot hard against a small oak stump. In spite of the acute pain, he forced himself to stand during the whole Paschal Matins. His legs, in pain due to standing every day in church for many years, already afflicted him. Now, from this injury and his efforts to stand afterwards, open sores developed. The doctors, eager to help, did not quite understand this sickness, and his legs were irritated by various compresses which caused severe inflammation, and later scurvy developed. No remedies were able to help them. For more than half a year the sick one was unable to leave his cell. Although there was some improvement, the disease remained incurable, and throughout the next thirty years it caused painful sufferings, which Fr. Anthony endured with amazing meekness. His state of mind was expressed in a letter to one of his relatives in Moscow, who became seriously ill at the same time:

"I have been consoling myself with the hope that I might have the pleasure of visiting you soon if I feel better. Yet, God disposes in different ways than we want. In the same way that your travels are only from one room to another, likewise, my trips are only from the stove-couch to the bench. But I am not as concerned about my own sickness as about your sufferings, since I know from the teachings of the Holy Fathers that every temptation or illness is sent to us by God as a cure for our infirm soul. For if our body suffers, God forgives our past and present sins and prevents us from sinning in the future. This is why we should wholeheartedly thank the Lord God Who is so merciful to us and turns everything to our benefit and permits us to be ill. Thus, we shouldn't grumble. This is the reason why I am trying, with the help of God, to endure my illness meekly. If my legs sometimes bother me, I endure it calmly. If my medication runs out, I don't let it disturb me. If I can't sit, I lie down. If my sides grow tired from lying on them, I get up without being annoyed. If something unpleasant happens to me, I try to bear it without becoming upset, because I myself have many times caused others pain, either knowingly or in ignorance. I eat any food served to me whether I like it or not; and for everything I thank God, especially for not depriving me of reading books and offering to Him my unworthy prayers. I have never had as much time for reading soul-profiting books as I have now in my prolonged illness, and therefore I wonder—how shall I thank my God for all that He has granted me!

"This is my state of mind during my sickness, and I have not concealed it from you. I don't know how it is with you. Maybe you carry your cross with more nobility of mind than I do, which would make me happy. When you in your grief are fainthearted from lack of patience, I am not surprised since it is part of our feeble nature to despond and grow faint under the burden of misfortunes. However, faintheartedness and lack of patience do not help in the least, but arouse greater depression. Because of all this, I ask you in the name of God to be as courageous as you can. Since we ourselves cannot acquire either patience, courage, or gratefulness—since these and other blessings do not come from people but are sent down to us by the Father of Lights—we have to lift our inner eyes up to Him Who dwells in Heaven and appeal to His goodness in this way: 'O Lord, Thou knowest what is profitable for me. I hope in Thee, O Lord, and entrust myself to Thy holy will. Deal with me as Thou wishest. If Thou wilt open to me the doors of Thy mercy, I shall be cured. Yet if it shall please Thee that I should further drink the bitter herbs of Thy judgments to drive off the perniciousness of sin, may it be blessed. Not my will but Thine be done! Only grant me Thy help in my grief, and be my refuge in all the tribulations which possess me. As Thou Thyself was tempted, so quickly grant me Thy help and steadfast patience with gratefulness in all my illnesses, misfortunes, afflictions, griefs, temptations, and needs of soul and body!' This is how the Hierarch of Christ, Demetrius [of Rostov] teaches us to pray in all sorrowful circumstances. And when you, in a similar manner, submit yourself to the will of God while being sick, I believe that the grace of God will hasten to visit you and grant peace to your soul and comfort to your heart, as well as relief to your body."

This is the way Fr. Anthony taught others to be patient. The spiritual power of his counsels shows that he gave them from his own experience and that he personally set the greatest example of patience in illness.

As soon as Fr. Anthony received some relief from his grave illness, he continued his previous task as the Superior of the Skete. But an even more difficult experience was awaiting him. Fr. Anthony did not faint under the burden of his unbelievable tasks, privations, and ascetic deeds. He magnanimously and with gratitude carried his cross in sickness, and the Lord, Who alone tries the reins and hearts of those He loves and grants unto all what is profitable, placed a new cross on him. It was a burden under which even such a courageous ascetic nearly collapsed. This cross was the rank of abbot.

On the 30th of November, 1839, His Eminence Nicholas, Bishop of Kaluga, unexpectedly summoned Fr. Anthony to Kaluga and on the 3rd of December appointed him Abbot of the Maloyaroslavets Black Island Monastery, which since the beginning of the century had received its abbots from the Optina Monastery. Fr. Anthony's parting from his spiritual family—with whom he had lived for eighteen years, first as a humble brother and later as a loving father—was touching. It was not easy for the ailing Elder to part from the beloved solitude of the Skete where he had hoped to end his life in peaceful prayer, but he remembered the saying of the Holy Fathers: "Obedience is greater than prayer and fasting." With many tears, with heartfelt grief and sorrow, yet with absolute submission, Fr. Anthony went to his assigned place, followed by the blessings and expressions of sincere spiritual love from the brotherhoods of both the Skete and the Monastery of Optina.

The entrance into the Optina Skete in the late 19th century, as it looked when Fr. Anthony, its superior, had to leave.

4

Abbacy in the St. Nicholas Monastery in Maloyaroslavets

1839-1853

BY GOD'S PROVIDENCE the three Putilov brothers were almost simultaneously the abbots of three well-known monasteries: the eldest, Moses, in the Optina Monastery; the second, Isaiah, in the monastery of Sarov; and Fr. Anthony in the monastery at Maloyaroslavets. The eldest of the three, Fr. Moses, seemed to be a born leader. The labors and sorrows of an abbot, which he experienced in greater abundance than the other brothers, he bore with an exceptional magnanimity and firmness, as if he did not even feel their weight, or at least did not show it. The other brothers often collapsed under the burden of being superiors. Thus, Fr. Isaiah, who served first as treasurer and later as abbot of Sarov Monastery, in letters to his brothers complained in powerful and moving language of the difficulty of bearing the burden which was placed on him.

"You mentioned," he wrote among other things, "two sisters, Martha and Mary, who served our Lord Jesus Christ. The zeal of both of them is praised by the Saviour. But I, following the example of Martha, am irritated with my duties in the Monastery in satisfying the bodily needs of the brethren, and deserve neither praise from God nor from men because I am not patient. It seems to me that in bustling around I work not for my salvation, but for my complete perdition. While a novice at the beginning of my departure from the world, I said within myself, 'The night is far spent, the day is at hand' (Rom. 13:12). Now I sing, 'The day is far spent, the night is at hand.' Thus, my dear brother, I have briefly described my pitiful situation...."

"I heard from one Elder that to be a founder is a martyrdom, but to be a treasurer is to be a publican; and this is entirely correct."

"We really don't know if we are saving others. Our own salvation while saving others becomes very doubtful, unless the exceptional mercy of God will save us who are in such endless bustling and care for external necessities. The experiences of holy men show how much external cares weaken our soul and totally divert our attention from God. I don't know about you, but because of my duties I do not have any free time, either during the day or at night, or on feast days or weekdays, to be free and attentive to myself...."

"The abbot is just like a human heart through which blood moves and circulates in a natural way. The day begins and he continually has to direct people, sending them to various obediences, and those capable are few. This is why our cross is so heavy. It seems to me that it is easier to be ill and suffer than to save others, because St. Arsenius the Great said that everyone has a different will, whereas in heaven the holy angels have the same unchanging will, to glorify God the Creator of all...."

"Being the superior under the present circumstances is a very burdensome task which can imperil one's salvation. How great was Moses, the leader of the Israelites! Yet even he sinned at the water of gainsaying, being led by the continuous murmuring of the people to doubt the power of God. Don't we see the same happening today as in ancient times? It seems even worse; only chattering and grumbling, sorrow and sighing are heard, which involuntarily makes even leaders waver and the strong grow weak. Perhaps the abbacy would be less dangerous among those whose hearts and souls are united, but that is very uncommon in this life...."

Fr. Isaiah concludes his complaints about his hardships as superior in the Christian spirit of obedience to the will of God: "It is true, the cross of leadership is not light. This is a difficulty which the aged Moses experienced. Jesus Christ strengthens us in such labors with these words: *Greater love hath no man than this, that a man lay down his life for his friends* (John 15:13). So, let us end our poor life with complete faith in our Lord God and Saviour Jesus Christ, Who suffered for our sake and rose again from the dead. He said in the Gospel: *He that believeth in Me, though he were dead, yet shall he live* (John 11:25)."

In fact, all the hardships of the abbacy described here were made even more difficult for Fr. Anthony by many other circumstances. After he had spent five years in the depths of the forest and eighteen years in the solitude of the Skete, Maloyaroslavets seemed to him like a noisy capital city, as he once admitted. It was not easy for him to get used to life in an urban monastery; and, what is more, it lay next to a highway. Besides that, Fr. Anthony was used to the strict rules of a unified monastic community, while the monastery of Maloyaroslavets was formed by the union of twelve monks from a vacant and lax state-supported monastery with seven brothers of the former monastic community. Furthermore, Abbot Anthony was suffering from acute pain in his legs and for a long time could not leave his cell. He was unable to actually observe everything that transpired in the monastery or personally give the necessary orders, and was therefore constrained to transmit his orders through others. It is understandable that this caused many difficulties and inconveniences. If one adds to all this the fact that Fr. Anthony was by nature more inclined to obey and continue his solitary life of silence than to command others, it is not surprising that he was exhausted from bearing the cross of abbot and often sank into deep depression.

In his letter to the Elders of the Optina Skete, Fr. Anthony described his arrival at the place of his appointment:

"If the holy Apostle Paul commands us to thank God for everything, then I, the unworthy one, should on my part thank God; and I am informing you, my fathers, that on the third day of December, thanks be to the Lord God, through the prayers of the Archbishop I was elevated to the rank of abbot. I received from his right hand the abbot's staff together with the chains, that is, the full weight of that yoke, and carried them with me to my monastery on the eve of the Feast of St. Nicholas. I arrived one-half hour before the beginning of Vespers, where the entire brotherhood met me at the gates with the Holy Cross, along with my own cross which I kissed with tears. This was my first honor. After several days I fell into despair. Then while dozing I beheld in a light sleep a choir of the Fathers, and one of them, like a hierarch, blessed me and said, 'You have been in Paradise and you know it; now work, pray, and don't be lazy!' And suddenly awakening, I felt peace within me. O Lord, grant me a blessed end!"*

The predecessor of Fr. Anthony, Archimandrite Macarius, rendered unforgettable services in the restoration and renovation of the monastery in Maloyaroslavets. Now that the outward Monastery was established, the inner foundation still had to be

---

* The Optina Elder Fr. Leonid, when Fr. Anthony related to him all the details of that dream, said that the God-pleaser whom he saw was St. Metrophanes of Voronezh, who took great care of him. In compliance with the command of the Elder, Fr. Anthony afterwards went on pilgrimage to Voronezh in order to venerate the holy relics of St. Metrophanes and to thank him for his care.

St. Nicholas Maloyaroslavets Monastery

arranged and strengthened in the spirit of faith and piety, according to the rules of the experienced ascetics and the examples of the best Russian monasteries. Abbot Anthony showed special zeal in this spiritual task while he was abbot in the holy Monastery, and as long as he was able he made himself an example of diligence and the strict fulfillment of all monastery duties.

"Many abbots," he wrote to a close friend in 1842, "do everything using someone else's hands, and I, a sinner, have to go to every church service, join in the reading and singing, eat together with the brethren, and so on. And last autumn I also helped to harvest cabbage in the vegetable garden, and this is the reason why I don't notice how fast time flies."

In his first years as abbot,* in addition to his regular duties, Fr. Anthony had to take care of finishing the interior decoration of the monastery church of St. Nicholas, the foundation of which had already been laid during the time of his predecessor. The consecration of this church took place in 1843, on the day of the commemoration of the battle of Borodino, the 26th of August. Fr. Anthony was unable to take part in the consecration, however, because immediately before it he became very ill. Here is how he described it:

"Glory be to God, our magnificent church was solemnly consecrated on August 26th by His Eminence Nicholas, together with other clergy. There were, like the number of the Apostles, twelve members of the clergy present: four abbots of monasteries, four archpriests, and four of lower rank. The festival was majestic and radiant. But the Lord did not bless me to take part in the service as I was quite sick, due to the many labors, cares, bustlings about, and management of expenses. That is why I, lying in bed, called upon the Lord from my sorrowing soul with tears, 'I see Thy bridal chamber, O my Saviour, but I have no garment to enter there....'"**

From the day of his appointment to Maloyaroslavets, Fr. Anthony was continually ill. Sometimes his ailments became severe, yet he endured them meekly and did not even care much about their treatment. In his sufferings he exclaimed from the bottom of his heart, "Blessed art Thou, O Lord Jesus, for Thy loving-kindness, glory to Thee!" Still, the abbacy weighed upon him, especially since his illness, as we previously mentioned, did not allow him to give his personal attention and orders in regards

* In 1842, the Metropolitan of Kiev, Philaret, passed through Maloyaroslavets. See the interesting excerpt from the personal calendar of Fr. Anthony in Part II, Chapter 4, p. 215.

** Stichera from the Lenten service during Passion Week.

to the monastery affairs, which resulted in some negligence. He wrote to his brother and Elder, Fr. Moses: "I grieve that, on account of my being the abbot, I bear the blame before God and men. I, myself, have many faults and weaknesses, but the faults of the brethren and their weaknesses sometimes weigh even more on me than my own."

He also wrote to a nun who found herself in a difficult situation: "Here I am the abbot—I live in a bright, warm, spacious cell, yet I have almost twice as many tribulations as you. It seems to me that I would rather like to move into a dark, damp cellar if only I could receive freedom from an abbot's martyric chains...."

"If you knew, my beloved daughter, how heavy is the cross those in authority bear, how bitter the cup they inwardly drink! It would be easier to accept daily insults and scourgings from men than the sufferings of being a superior in our day. And how we will have to account for everything in the future age! For he who has received much will have to account for much; and if one can hardly save his own soul, can it be easier to save the souls of others? Judge for yourself! Thus, know only this: save yourself and this will already be enough for you."

These were the thoughts and feelings of Fr. Anthony while he bore the burden of his duty. In 1843, after he had finished the task that had been worrying the Archbishop and himself for a long time—that is, the consecration of the St. Nicholas church and the building and decoration of it (which had lasted for thirty years)—Fr. Anthony tried for the first time to relieve himself of the responsibilities of abbot. This was prompted by rumors that some high authorities in Petersburg intended to appoint Fr. Anthony the abbot of a reestablished monastery in a certain diocese. Because of this, he first addressed his spiritual father and brother according to the flesh, Fr. Moses, asking for his blessing to carry out his intention. Fr. Anthony wrote to him, unburdening before him his deep and heartfelt grief in a humble and contrite spirit: "I confess to you, Father, that although I have spent my life like a brute beast, it sometimes scares me to die as an animal, that is, without the thought of death and without preparing for my departure. That is why I wish to move close to you, if it is the will of God, in order to amend my life during the days that remain, so that instead of two mites I may offer to the Lord a contrite and humble heart—for this reason I ask your holy prayers." Fr. Moses gave his consent to the desire of Fr. Anthony and blessed him to act according to his inner conviction. Next, Fr. Anthony addressed his petition to His Eminence Nicholas, asking him to permit him to retire to the Optina Monastery, but after a certain time he received the following reply:

"Most venerable Father, Abbot Anthony! Your letter of September 20th made it very difficult for me to comply with your request. Moreover, the rumors about your potential pro-motion further induce me to silence. Finally, I can't conceal from you my feelings and thoughts in connection with your wish. The elders in former times and similar instances said, together with the royal prophet, *I will chant unto my God as long as I have my being.* If they were afflicted by an illness perhaps even worse than yours, they believed like the Apostle Paul that the power of God is made perfect in weakness. I recommend that you also follow the example of these Godly-wise men. Spare me the duty of choosing a new abbot to replace you. I assure you emphatically that I have no such person in mind. If your illness is dangerous, go to the best hospital in Moscow or to your relatives there and let skilled doctors treat you. Even our Lord God forbids us to refuse the treatment of a wise doctor. Don't worry too much about your monastery during your absence, or in case of a prolonged illness. He Who directs all things will preserve it in due order, knowing the diligence and good

ABBACY IN THE ST. NICHOLAS MONASTERY

intentions of the abbot. This is my advice to you! However, it
depends on your will to follow it. Every human being has been
created free in his thoughts, will, and even actions. May the Lord
maintain your strength! I pray for this. Nicholas, Bishop of
Kaluga. 1843, the 26th day of October. Kaluga."

Fr. Anthony was distressed upon receiving such a reply. His
desire to cast off the chains of abbacy was so strong that he went
to Kaluga in order to personally ask the Bishop to relieve him,
but he did not obtain what he desired. He was received by the
Bishop very favorably. As for being discharged from his duty,
the Bishop decidedly told him that even if he had to lie
motionless in bed for two years, he still would not be replaced;
not only should he not seek means to be released from his duties,
but he should not even think about it. Hearing such a resolute
reply, Fr. Anthony was hardly able to refrain from crying. He
said to the Bishop, "If death should befall me, then your
archpastor's heart will be ridden with grief that, having the
liberty and opportunity to grant me leave from my duty, you
didn't grant me this favor." "Let this sin burden my soul,"
answered the Bishop.

After such a refusal, the Bishop, according to the expression
of Fr. Anthony, consoled him like an infant. They walked
together around Kaluga for almost an hour; the Bishop showed
him the homes and buildings and, upon returning, detained
him until midnight. Finally, knowing that the greatest consolation for Fr. Anthony would be to visit his Elder, he offered to
take him to Optina. But the distressed Fr. Anthony did not want
to go there, and from Kaluga returned directly to his Monastery.

All of Fr. Anthony's letters written during this period to his
elder brother are full of deep sorrow. Following are some
excerpts from them:

"I received your pleasant letter in which you bless me to
continue to bear my burden with trust in the power of God,

and so I submit myself to God's will and yours. However, I confess to you my weakness that almost every day I fall into depression beneath the burden of my position. The Bishop's persuasion may be reasonable; but if someone is sinking into an abyss, then at that moment saving help is needed rather than the persuasion that drowning will be beneficial. I thank you deeply for your letter and encouragement for me who am desponding...."

"Forgive me, Batiushka, for the Lord's sake," he wrote in another letter, "for my injudicious plans. I well know that these bad thoughts issue from my heart, but what can I do? It would be better for me to bear the burden placed on me as a dumb animal does, bearing it silently until I collapse, but I am still far from reaching that [spiritual] level. If during bodily illness it is allowed to use different measures for relief, then since my soul suffers more, should I not likewise take care of my soul? My physical ailments have almost never stopped bothering me, and if our Lord God wants to add yet more, His will be done! However, although I am trying to find relief, if God will not deliver me, can a man deliver me? In the beginning I thought that I would be unable to live even a year in Maloyaroslavets, but I have lived here five years. Even now, I know not what awaits me in the future. I am asking you to do me a favor by interceding for me in your prayers to God and also persuading me to listen to reason."

He again wrote: "I ask you humbly to magnanimously forgive my former and present faintheartedness. What am I to do? The sadness of my heart does not leave me. It seems that I have to end my life in sickness of body and soul. Although this is very hard for me at the present time, I can find neither relief nor consolation. *There is no peace in my bones in the face of my sins* (Psalm 37:3). As a priest I proclaim peace to others, yet I can't give myself any; therefore my soul is deeply troubled."

In 1844, Fr. Anthony again submitted his application to the Bishop to be relieved of his responsibilities. In this petition he explained that during the course of the year he compelled himself to continue his work and his health had not improved; on the contrary, in addition to the pre-existing incurable affliction of his legs, he was afflicted by other illnesses: dizziness, fainting spells and shortness of breath. He further explained that his poor condition was deteriorating because the many disorders in the Monastery disturbed him, the number of which might increase in the future by reason of his poor health. This would affect the morale of the brethren as well as the economic management of the Monastery, for which the head of the Monastery would have to answer to God and to the Bishop.

He wrote: "Since I have no hope of improving in order to manage the Monastery entrusted to me, I lose even more courage and effectiveness, which are necessary to perform my duty; and because of this the Monastery will surely fall into worse disorder. This is the reason why I throw myself at the feet of Your Eminence, imploring you with tears to hearken to my infirm voice, to be considerate to me and release me from my duty—permit me to go to Optina Monastery in order to restore my spiritual and physical strength. I am weak in soul and body, yet I do not dare to say, *'I have no one to help me'* (John 5:7).* I have you, merciful Archpastor! Your affirmative reply to my voice of pain would be the remedy of relief from the weakness of my soul. As the widow crying out to the unjust judge was avenged, I trust even more in you who are rightly dividing the word of truth and who have already granted me so many favors as Bishop and father." But the Bishop's answer to this tearful petition was very short:

---

* The words of the paralytic at the sheep's pool.

"It is not the appropriate time for you to request your retirement from the abbacy, nor for me to choose someone else to replace you. You and I have work to do. On the occasion of the unveiling of the memorial (in Maloyaroslavets) on the 29th of October, according to the will of the Sovereign Emperor, I have to be present at the celebration. Give orders for cells to be prepared," and so on.

Fr. Anthony submitted himself to the will of the Bishop, but he still suffered spiritually every day and wondered if the Lord might perhaps release him from his sufferings. He was always searching for a way to be relieved of his duties. At that time, he received through some devoted persons an invitation to transfer to the newly established Gethsemane Skete. Fr. Anthony loved the Optina Monastery and wished to be with his spiritual father and Elder, Moses; but the burden of being abbot weighed heavily upon him, and he uttered these words: "If I could obtain the consent and blessing of my spiritual father (that is, Fr. Moses), I would consider this transfer to be the will of God and would undoubtedly go."

When Fr. Anthony explained to Fr. Moses the decision he had made, he obtained a very strict and even threatening reply. Fr. Moses wrote: "Since I am sincerely taking part in the direction of your life, anything pleasant gives me consolation, and anything to the contrary upsets me, especially those things concerning God which are against His will. From your letter, among some pleasant things I learned also about your unforgivable intention to abandon your duty which was laid on you from the Lord Himself through our Archpastor, by which action you would insult the holy Monastery entrusted to you. It would grieve the Bishop, the Lord Himself, and would grieve my sinful self and my Monastery as well, and place you in the grave before your time. Our common enemy, the devil, desires this. You, seeking for deliverance from your sorrows, are expressing your own will against the most holy will of God and are sinfully placing me in a position against people of importance. I do not agree with your impure will, and I submit myself completely to the will of God and am afraid to think differently. I did not elevate you to the rank which you now have. The Lord so established you through hierarchical authority and entrusted you with the Monastery, and He will keep you steadfast to do the work of God until your death. The holy Apostle admonishes us to do the same: *Let this mind be in you, which was also in Christ Jesus, Who … became obedient unto death, even the death of the cross* (Phil. 2:5,6,8). *Let us run with patience the race that is set before us, looking unto Jesus the author and finisher of our faith* (Heb. 12:1-2). *Many are the tribulations of the righteous, and the Lord shall deliver them out of them all* (Psalm 33:19). I assuredly tell you, my beloved, and affirm it in the name of our Lord Jesus, from this moment forth stop the grumbling complaints about your duty. It is not an evil but a great good. Despondency and evasion of your duty, following the counsel of that pernicious spirit, shows that you are still living neither with the right mind nor faith. One has to be one in spirit with the Lord; with Him there is no room for despondency. This is why the holy Apostle, encouraging the ascetic to labor, says: *Brethren be strong in the Lord and in the power of His might* (Eph. 6:10). *In your patience possess ye your souls* (Luke 21:19), and *He that endureth to the end shall be saved,* says the Lord (Matt. 10:22). From the bottom of my heart I wish that you would follow not your will nor my will, but only the will of God to Whom I entrust myself and you with your entire Monastery, remaining yours with sincere love."

Thus wrote Fr. Moses, knowing that Fr. Anthony accepted everything from him with faith and humility. "I sense the total fairness of your words," he replied to his brother, "but could not accept them without pain of heart. Of course, if you felt with your heart my poor situation, you would feel sorry for me. It doesn't cause me much grief and woe to sacrifice my peace, to experience spiritual disturbance, or to sacrifice even the salvation of my soul, but since I am abbot, everything else leads to (or has already resulted in) disorder and disaster in my soul. Hence by leaving my duty I would cause damage only to myself, while remaining here I may destroy and lead others into perdition, which has already happened in some cases. But if you have decided that I must remain silent and not grumble about my duty, I will obediently submit myself to your will and by your holy prayers I will be silent, only confessing my grief to God."

And Fr. Anthony actually did become silent and remained in silence about one and a half years, and only after that time did he decide to pour out again before his brother his constant grief. "If we see," he wrote, "that our novices are fainting beneath their burden, our hearts are touched, and often we make some allowance for them or even completely release them from their load. Is it possible that your paternal heart can be hardened to my sufferings? Have mercy on me for God's sake! Here I have continued, out of obedience to your holy will, to carry the heavy burden of the abbacy with great effort for almost seven years; and if I had never seen examples of someone resigning from his duties in ancient times as well as in recent times, I would have never dared to think, let alone ask, for my release. I have been hoping that you might open unto me your fatherly embrace as for a prodigal son and forgive me who am ailing in soul and body; but you have sentenced me to suffer without end. What can I do? Although this decision pains my heart, still I have to suffer and be tormented. Be it unto me according to God's will and yours."

With such willpower, obedience and patience, Fr. Anthony bore the spiritual cross placed on him by God Himself. And finally the Lord took care of his patient servant, that is, He granted him some inner consolation, although He still did not release him from the duties of abbot.

Fr. Moses replied to the letter of Fr. Anthony in this manner: "Dearest brother! *Be strong in the Lord and in the power of His might* (Eph. 6:10). If you remain silent and patient, no doubt you will see God's help. Since He alone knows all, entrust yourself to Him without any doubt. It is God Who takes care of His creation and saves people from all temptations. If the soul abides where it desires to be and not where the body resides, then your soul with love will abide with us in Optina Monastery. In the same way, my soul with love is not separated from you in your Black Island Monastery; it speaks to you through my thoughts and, at times, face to face, and offers sincere hopefulness to the Lord, asking Him to grant you the strength to bear the grief of your duty placed upon you as a cross. And I believe and hope that the Lord will not abandon you. Spiritual dejection is unavoidable; only patience and prayer can overcome it. Likewise pernicious sadness of heart, which is explained by St. Cassian in the fourth volume of the *Philokalia*,* needs to be cured."

By the mercy of God and through the great faith with which Fr. Anthony accepted every word of his Elder, this letter put an end to the grievous sufferings of his soul. "Your dearest letter, like a healing balm, brought some relief to my sufferings. Since then I have begun to calm myself by remembering your promise of deliverance. I also previously believed your holy words; but I was so ailing in spirit that there was nothing that was able to calm me save your last letter. Because of that, I first thanked the Lord with tears of gratitude from the bottom of my heart, and then sincerely thanked you with a prostration, my gracious

---

* Volume One in the English translation of the Greek *Philokalia.*

father, for instructing me in my distress, and I ask you not to deprive me of your instruction in the future."*

The abbacy of Fr. Anthony lasted about seven more years. During this time, although he felt burdened in his heart with the management of the Monastery while being so ill, his grief no longer reached a state of oppressive despondency, and he was not so exhausted under the load of his cross, carrying it with greater meekness.

It should be mentioned that not only in the last years, but also previously when Fr. Anthony had been greatly depressed in spirit, he did not manifest it in his outward activity and his dealing with people. He always cordially welcomed visitors. Even in times of severe anguish of soul, his conversation was lively, and he was always ready to listen with concern and sympathy to the troubles of anyone who confided his sorrow of heart to him. In return, he would personally console each one or write letters of counsel, full of spiritual power. He did not reveal to many people the sorrow of his own heart. He was sincerely hospitable and conscientiously carried out his duty as abbot for everyone. He also watched carefully that the church services were conducted in due order and personally celebrated with great zeal, even while ill, the festive services on the great feasts.

While Fr. Anthony was abbot, in addition to the other church services, two Liturgies were served daily without fail— one in the early morning and the second one later. With special zeal and punctuality, prayers were read for the monastery benefactors. On the patronal feast of the Church of St. Nicholas on

---

* About the same time, Fr. Anthony received from his Elder, as a consolation and blessing, an icon of our Saviour which he especially revered until his death, always remembering with gratitude that, since receiving the icon, his sorrow of many years had ceased.

the 9th of May, the service lasted six hours, during which time Fr. Anthony would always read the *ikosi* to the Saint before reading the Gospel. Before Liturgy he would serve a moleben himself with the blessing of water, then concelebrate the Liturgy, and afterwards serve a moleben to the Saint. At the end of the service he would receive guests and the brethren in his cell and personally serve them all. Then, toward evening, he would rush by postal carriage to Kaluga in order to congratulate Bishop Nicholas on his nameday.

In 1848, when Maloyaroslavets was plagued by an epidemic of cholera, Fr. Anthony, complying with the request of the people, went several times with all the clergy in procession around the entire city. Together they served many molebens and litanies for the dead, as well as *panikhidas* for the soldiers who perished there in 1812. Each time the procession would last about seven hours. Such labors Fr. Anthony endured on his ailing legs.

With zeal Abbot Anthony similarly watched over the welfare of the Monastery and its external and internal affairs, through his own counsel and utilizing the help of chosen experienced spiritual fathers. With personal exhortations and with all possible means, they strove together to strengthen in the brethren good morality and behavior. After he had laid the firm foundation of the internal composition of the Monastery, Fr. Anthony finished the external construction which had been initiated by his predecessor. This required still further labor and great expense in view of the stark finances of the Monastery.

In February, 1849, there was a violent storm in Maloyaroslavets. The wind knocked down the spire of the belltower, which fell on the church and by its weight crushed the iron roof, rafters, and the stone arches. The iron cross was blown into the garden 120 yards away. This storm caused 5,000 roubles worth of damage in the Monastery, yet Fr. Anthony did not worry about the damage, laying his grief before the Lord God and His most pure Mother, and the great Wonderworker, St. Nicholas. He only thanked God that no one was hurt during the storm. A layman, hearing this story from Fr. Anthony, was startled by his complete indifference towards the material damage and his sincere joy concerning the preservation of the lives of all who lived in the Monastery. In thinking about it, he realized that the Abbot valued the life of the least monastic laborer more than the 5,000 roubles. When he expressed this thought to Fr. Anthony, the latter remarked that a human soul is more precious to God than all the things in this world.

Although in this case Fr. Anthony placed all his hope in God's Providence, the pressing and rapid completion of the adornment of the monastery church could not but trouble and burden him. He was a poor collector of money. He not only did not like to solicit it, but even refused to take the money someone offered if he saw that he donated more than he could possibly afford in his situation. Fr. Anthony would try to convince him to take part of it back. However, according to the will of the Bishop, Fr. Anthony had to go to the capital to solicit donations, and, with the Lord's help, in 1849 he finished the exterior adornment of the Maloyaroslavets Monastery initiated by his predecessor, making it look the way it now appears [1870]. At the consecration in 1840 of the newly constructed Church of the Transfiguration, a great celebration was held in the Monastery which the Bishop attended. Many people recall that Fr. Anthony seated Emilian, a fool-for-Christ well known in Maloyaroslavets, next to himself at the table, and afterwards said that "two fools were sitting next to each other."

All the labors, tribulations, and great care shown by Fr. Anthony in performing the duties of Superior, while he was exhausted beneath the burden of his own inner cross, were well understood and appreciated by the Bishop who kept him at his

The Three Pillars of Optina: Saints Anthony, Moses and Macarius.

duty. Already in 1845, at the recommendation of the Bishop, Fr. Anthony was awarded the gold pectoral cross. Informing him about this award, Bishop Nicholas wrote to him: "You are doing the right thing in refusing all secular decorations. But His Majesty the Emperor, at the recommendation of the Holy Synod, awarded you this cross on the 21st of April. This is not a secular decoration, but the symbol of the sufferings of our Redeemer, our Lord God and Saviour Jesus Christ. You have to accept this spiritual, Christian and saving distinction. Let it be at the same time the mark of your physical and mental sorrows. But is there really anyone in this world who does not have them?" Later the Bishop wanted to recommend that the Holy Synod elevate Fr. Anthony to the rank of archimandrite; but when Fr. Anthony heard of it, he convinced the Bishop to abandon this plan, speaking to him in this way: "If the dignity of archimandrite would save me from decay, death, or condemnation, then it would be worthwhile to desire it."

During the entire time which Fr. Anthony spent living in Maloyaroslavets, Fr. Moses gave him great support, sincere brotherly love, and, at the same time, fatherly assistance in his work. Fr. Anthony, being already an abbot, never ceased being a perfect novice with regard to his brother. He always corresponded with him, sharing all his tribulations, doubts and plans, and asked for his blessing and approval for everything. He never undertook anything without his consent. Fr. Moses, on his part, not only assisted him and supported him by his experienced counsel, directions and admonitions, but also took an active part in helping him in his work. Several times when Maloyaroslavets Monastery did not have enough brethren, more were sent from Optina Monastery on obedience. To the great regret of Abbot Anthony, some brethren, due to their inconstancy or for some other reason, suddenly left after staying in the Monastery as long as they pleased, and the Monastery was deprived of the most necessary people in the brotherhood. The Abbot did not detain anyone who wanted to leave the Monastery.*

In general, a brotherly relationship had always existed between the two monasteries in Maloyaroslavets and Optina. Fr. Moses also visited his brother every year in Maloyaroslavets. These visits were the happiest moments for Fr. Anthony, as he could unburden his heart before his Elder and tell him about his grief. He was able to personally explain to him all matters and conditions which needed to be resolved, and from these conversations came the strength to continue his very difficult obedience. Fr. Anthony also went every year to Optina Monastery for a short rest.

Sometimes Fr. Anthony went to Moscow, as previously stated, to collect donations for the completion of the monastery buildings and for some other monastery projects as well. There in 1850 and in 1851 he met his brothers, Basil, who was living in Rostov, and Fr. Isaiah, who was the abbot in Sarov. He had

---

* As one example, we offer a curious excerpt from Fr. Anthony's letter to the Bishop written about such a case: "According to the request of Your Eminence, with due obedience I am reporting by the first post the following: I have not sent away from the Monastery my former secretary, I. A. It was his own wish to move to another monastery, and I don't see any other reason for it except for my disorderly life and my blameworthy weaknesses which I couldn't hide from him. However, I advised him not to be in a hurry and gave him a chance to think it over and take counsel with some of the more sensible brethren. In spite of this, he didn't change his intention, and so I let him go peacefully and provided him with money and transportation to Kaluga. Yet, I couldn't persuade myself to take him back again, although I was moved by his sincere repentance. This I did not because of caprice, but because it would not be of benefit to his soul (to return) since I have not changed at all. Besides, what kind of life would a novice have if he thought of his abbot as a bear and was always afraid of being crushed to death by him. This is the reason why I advised him to go ahead with his plan and not to look back."

Bishop Gregory of Kaluga

not seen the former in twenty-one years and the latter in thirty-three years. In Moscow, Fr. Anthony was always honored by the blessing and attention of the Metropolitan of Moscow [Philaret]. The Elder-Metropolitan understood the spirituality of the humble suffering ascetic and came to love him. He often invited him to serve with him and showed him other expressions of paternal kindness. By his wise conversations he gave him comfort and encouragement for his hard work; and, finally, co-suffering with his situation, he felt sympathy for him and interceded for him with the Bishop of Kaluga by requesting that Fr. Anthony be discharged from his duty. As a result of this intercession, in 1851 Bishop Nicholas agreed to give consideration to the long-standing petition of the suffering abbot. However, the sudden death of the Bishop again interrupted this action. Then, the present Bishop of Kaluga [Gregory], respecting the intercession of the Metropolitan of Moscow and taking into consideration Fr. Anthony's ailments, relieved him of the abbacy and allowed him to retire to Optina Monastery.

In Abbot Anthony's notebook the following is written:

"On the 9th of February, 1853, I, the unworthy Abbot Anthony, passed on the leadership of the St. Nicholas Black Island Monastery in Maloyaroslavets to the new Father Superior, Abbot Nicodemus. After serving a moleben of thanksgiving to the Lord God for all His past benefits unto me and for His protection of my thirteen years' sojourn in Maloyaroslavets, I asked all the brethren for forgiveness and left the Monastery at one o'clock in the afternoon. On the 12th, I arrived at the God-preserved Optina Monastery where I was paternally received. O Lord, bless my entrance into this holy Monastery and grant me a good end therein, by the prayers of my holy Father."

Return through the Skete gates. The path into the cloistered Skete church as it looked during Fr. Anthony's time and as it looks today.

5

Life in Retirement at Optina Monastery

1853-1865

AFTER HIS ARRIVAL at Optina Monastery, Abbot Anthony wrote in a letter to one of his spiritual children: "By the mercy of God and through the holy supplications of those praying for me, I passed through Kaluga safely with only one ten-kopeck piece, and arrived at Optina Monastery to retire on February 12th. I was received by my dear Father, Abbot Moses in a very paternal way, in the true sense of the word, that is, with love and kindness. On the occasion of my return he arranged a gathering like the celebration for the lost piece of silver which was found. Batiushka let me have a warm cell close to his own, from which I could see only the sky, and gazing thereat I cry out from the depths of my soul: *Unto thee have I lifted up mine eyes, unto Thee that dwellest in heaven. Behold, as the eyes of servants look unto the hands of their masters ... so do our eyes look unto the Lord our God, until He take pity on us* (Psalm 122:1-2). I'm unable to find the proper words to express my gratitude for God's mercy toward me. In truth the Lord God has recompensed me not according to my sins, but according to His great mercy and the multitude of His compassions." The joy of Fr.

Anthony's present life was heightened by the remembrance of all the sorrows he had experienced before.

In 1856, he wrote in his notebook, "It became clear to me that my life as abbot for thirteen years in the Monastery in Maloyaroslavets, where I had to suffer many temptations and afflictions, did me much good. Without it I would not welcome and appreciate so greatly my peaceful life here. I am unable to thank God enough for bringing me back to my former dwelling in the Optina Monastery."

The peace for which Abbot Anthony had been longing, and which was to last until his blessed repose, was nevertheless filled with labors and illnesses; yet, in a spiritual sense, it was very fruitful. He had been longing for deliverance from his abbatical duties not just for his own peace, but because it neither agreed with his spiritual disposition nor his physical strength. This was why he, when released according to his wish, devoted himself to the work of God with great zeal like a beginner, and with great patience continued to bear the involuntary cross of illness.

"My present life, thanks to the Lord God," he wrote in April of 1853, "is pleasant and peaceful, yet it exhausts me very much on account of various ailments, especially the increasing pain in my legs and teeth; however, all this is not without benefit for me. Although my body is ailing because of my sins and my soul is also suffering, I have, thanks to the Lord our God, strength to go every day to each service in the holy church and to stand there from the beginning to the end. I likewise go daily to the monastery refectory, where I now go not because it is my duty, but out of my own free will. This brings me such great benefit and consolation that every piece of simple food seems to me as sweet as sugar. I don't keep anything in my cell except holy water, so that not only people, but even poor mice have nothing on which to feast. No one visits me, and I live just like in the desert. Dear God! Let it be like that in the future, too! The only

The beloved entrance into the Skete and the Skete Church.

Inside: the Skete refectory as it looked during Elder Anthony's time.

thing that bothers me is my ailing legs, which do not comply with my wish to work all the time."

In such a state of mind Fr. Anthony began his life in retirement. In a short time the ailment of his legs, which had begun in 1836 as mentioned above, increased to such an extent, because of his excessive effort of standing for a long time, that he was covered with wounds up to his knees. Once during the all-night vigil, so much fluid issued from Fr. Anthony's wounds that his new leather boots were soaked as if he had been standing in water up to his knees. After that the wounds closed, but the pain became more acute because the pus, for which the wounds had served as a natural channel, remained inside. Some time after the wounds had closed, a novice who was passing by Fr. Anthony's cell saw him lying on the floor unconscious and covered with blood. Because of his closed wounds, Fr. Anthony had fainted, and in falling down had injured both of his ailing legs. Later, the wounds opened again, and a different kind of suffering began. We will not describe all the stages of his afflictions, but will only say in short that this illness lasted until the repose of the Elder, that is, for about thirty years. Every day and night the Elder suffered from indescribable pain in his legs, as if someone was at the same time cutting them with a knife, burning them with fire, severely scratching them with a brush, and pricking them with needles. One was unable to look at them without shuddering. His aching legs became hard like wood, and looked more like straight round logs, nine inches in diameter, dark red and inflamed. Out of the wounds, which were open deep down to the bone, the bloody fluid continually oozed. Dr. A. I. L. stated that while bandaging his legs he saw in the wounds worms one inch long.

Many doctors and visitors suggested remedies. Sometimes the Elder felt temporary relief and a little comfort from these remedies. For instance, they enabled him to touch his afflicted

Inside the Skete—the cell of Elder Anthony,
the Abbot of the Skete.

legs while changing bandages, whereas usually even a light touch was unbearable because of their excessive irritability. In general, none of the remedies were able to bring much relief, while some of them, instead of relief, caused harm. But Fr. Anthony did not contradict anyone nor refuse any treatment, even though he understood that his illness was incurable. He did not dwell on the fact that his sickness had been caused and made worse by his efforts to perform ascetic labors. Rather, he considered his sufferings as trials sent to him for the benefit of his soul in order to be cleansed of his sins. One day, the famous and pious writer I. V. Kireyevsky visited him and in talking to him expressed his thought this way: "By your example, Father, the words of Scripture are being proved that the righteous are sent much grief. What a heavy cross the Lord has placed on you!" "That's true," agreed the Elder, "the righteous are sent sorrows, but I have been sent all kinds of wounds, as the holy Prophet David said: *Many are the scourges of the sinner*" (Psalm 31:10).

For such great humility the Lord helped him to endure these awful sufferings by granting him courageous patience and marvelous meekness. When the pains grew too severe, he liked to remember Righteous Job and used to say as a consolation to others and to himself that all his sufferings were not worth even one sigh of that long-suffering martyr from the Old Testament. As if unaware of his own long-suffering, Fr. Anthony, while comforting one of his spiritual children who was in a painful situation, once expressed himself this way: "With my whole heart I feel sorry that you have to go through so many trials, but at the same time I envy you because the Lord loves you so much. The Lord sees your troubles and hears your heartfelt sighs. If you only knew how many rewards and ineffable consolations He has prepared for you! And I, a poor cripple, have not many wounds, and even these seem unbearable to me at times. Woe to me, the wretched one! I will be left empty-handed."

The Elder did not complain of his sufferings to God or to man. Many people, looking at his ever-radiant face and listening to his lively discourses, did not realize what a sufferer they had in front of them. Some, seeing his full stature, thought that he was quite healthy and only pretended to be ill.* It is not surprising. To people in the world, who even in the case of a minor illness think and care only for their peaceful rest, the patience of the Elder must have appeared inconceivable and incomprehensible. Fr. Anthony made a great effort, even when his sufferings were extreme, to greet very kindly and with a cheerful countenance not only people coming for spiritual instruction, but also visitors to the Monastery in general. He would sit and speak with them, patiently listening when they talked about things which were not important to anyone, neither to them nor to him, and would bid them farewell with the best wishes. Who among such visitors, departing after such a loving reception, consoled and cheered by Fr. Anthony, could ever imagine that the Elder, after having accompanied the departing guests out, often returned to his cell with great effort and groaning from pain? Fr. Anthony was ready to receive the next visitor with the same kindness, in spite of the fact that such efforts caused his sufferings to increase.

More and more, the Elder forced himself to prayerful labors for the sake of the love of God. In spite of his continual bodily sufferings, he liked to go to church on feast days as well as weekdays without fail, and always tried to arrive before the service began. Anyone would be touched in seeing how the ailing Elder at the first strike of the church bell would walk to church, barely able to move his feet and leaning upon his cane, and would stand during almost the entire service, as long as he

---

* Someone who visited Fr. Anthony described him as a most healthy man. Another said right to his face, "Half of Moscow is full of such 'saints' as you."

was able. Only when he felt exhausted would he sit down and then again, with hardship and groaning from pain, return to his cell.

Fr. Anthony especially cherished the Skete where he lived for eighteen years. On the days on which, according to the Skete *typicon,* there were festive church services, he always came to the Skete Liturgy in spite of his illness, leaving his cell an hour or more before the bells started to ring. In the Monastery on great feasts he sometimes even concelebrated the services, although this was beyond his strength; but in the last years he only attended them. After a long feast-day service the Archimandrite sometimes assigned him to do the spiritual reading during the brethren's meal in the refectory, and after that Fr. Anthony would remain to eat the meal served for the brethren who worked in the kitchen and refectory.

Sometimes such long standing on his ailing feet caused inflammation, and the Elder could not leave his cell for a whole month or more. In such cases he had to substitute his cell rule for church services. At night when the chime of the church bells called the brethren to the Midnight Service and Matins, those who were passing by Fr. Anthony's window could always see bright light in his cell. If he was unable to be present in church, the Elder without fail would read his rule of prayer in his cell at the same time as the service in church, as if he were not ill. His ascetic labors in his cell were known only to God. We can only guess and try to imagine them by his obvious great zeal and care for the church services, by the peaceful spiritual joy which radiated from him, and which was noticed by many people, and, thirdly, by his verbal admonitions. He used to say, "One should hurry to rise for prayer as if to a fire."

He wrote to one of his spiritual children when sending him a prayer rope: "Pray fervently to the Lord God and your cold heart will be warmed by His sweetest Name, for our God is Fire.

Calling upon His Name destroys impure thoughts and also warms our hearts to fulfill all His commandments." He said frankly to one close spiritual son that he was always praying, praying for each and everyone, and that when he was a superior he did not even come out to talk to workers who arrived for monastery business without preparing first by prayer. Some people noticed that while he was talking to visitors, he was also praying inwardly. God alone knows what spiritual heights Fr. Anthony reached through his prayers and what spiritual gifts he was granted. Only those who are experienced in the spiritual life can understand how to see their manifestation in others. We must limit ourselves to the few fragments, hints, and indications which we have seen and heard.

All who saw Fr. Anthony celebrating Divine Liturgy remember the unusual expression on his face, especially during the Grand Entrance with the chalice. His was the face of a man full of grace. It happened that, by merely looking at him at such times, several felt in their soul a moral transformation. There are substantial grounds on which to maintain that Fr. Anthony had great boldness in his prayers to God and was granted spiritual visions and other grace-filled visitations.* He had such

---

* A novice of the Optina Monastery, P., Fr. Anthony's spiritual son, told us: "On November 8th, 1862, on the commemoration of the Archangel Michael, before Matins I heard in a dream an unknown voice telling me, 'Your Elder, Fr. Anthony, lives a holy life and is a great Elder of God.' Right after that the bell rang, and therefore all the words said by the mysterious voice became clearly imprinted in my memory. Meditating upon what I heard, I went to Matins. I passed by close to the building where the Elder lived and saw the cell where Fr. Anthony prayed. Out of nowhere there appeared a bright white, fiery cloud nearly eight feet long and about five feet wide; quietly and slowly it began to rise from the roof and disappeared in the heavenly region of the sky. This appearance startled me, and returning from Matins I wrote it down for remembrance. I didn't dare to tell the Elder about it, but considered the vision as teaching me, the unworthy one, to have faith,

flaming zeal and pious love for the Mother of God that, especially in the last years of his life, when he began to say something about her life or even when he remembered the name of the most blessed Virgin Mary, his voice changed from the abundance of his tears and he would be unable to finish his story. However, he carefully hid his spiritual gifts from everyone.

When one of Fr. Anthony's closest spiritual sons whom he especially cherished would ask him about abstract matters, Fr. Anthony would answer that he did not understand anything about them and would send him either to the Elder Fr. Macarius or to Archimandrite Moses. They would sometimes give him answers, but at times they, too, would simply dismiss him without an answer. "Purify your heart and you will know everything," argued Fr. Macarius in answering his probing questions; but Fr. Moses in such cases always said the same thing: "This is a spiritual matter," and with that the conversation ended. Obviously, Abbot Anthony avoided conversations about abstract matters because he wanted to guide people to the active virtues, expressing in this way the heights of his humility. No matter what someone said or did, Fr. Anthony was never tempted to criticize or blame him; he never changed his good opinion of that individual, but looked at everyone and everything with a pure gaze, thereby proving that he had acquired a pure heart.

After prayers in church and in his cell, Fr. Anthony devoted his free time primarily to reading, which was his favorite occupation throughout his entire life. It would be difficult to find someone who loved to read as much as Fr. Anthony. In addition to the Holy Scriptures and the works of the Holy Fathers, especially the ascetic writings which chiefly nourished his soul,

---

devotion and obedience to my Elder, and as clear evidence of his pure, flaming and God-pleasing prayers.

the inquisitive Elder also read other spiritual and scholarly books. He loved first of all historical ones, and he could find good, salutary and useful things for himself and others in books which others paid little attention to. He always watched for advertisements from booksellers, wrote down the titles of books which he had not yet read, and occasionally tried to buy them. His spiritual children and acquaintances often presented him with different books, since they knew that no other gift would bring him as much consolation as some new book. If he would ever receive a monetary gift, the greater part went to acquiring books. In this way he eventually collected an extraordinary private library. If a book was hard to find, he would patiently, sometimes for years, try to find it.* While he was yet alive the Elder gave all his books, more than 2,000 volumes, to the monastery library. Being very conscientious in everything, he first took care to see that each book was bound. It is remarkable that Fr. Anthony did not leave unread a single one of the amazing quantity of books he donated.

Preserving his meek disposition and cheerful spirit in the midst of his great sufferings during his illnesses, while other people often lose the capacity to do anything, he found even more time for reading. He read much and he read attentively. In his youth he had acquired the habit of taking notes and excerpts from every book he read. Articles of interest or spiritual books rarely available in bookstores he personally copied out or gave for copying to his spiritual children. In this way, in addition to the manuscript collection which he compiled together with Fr. Moses in the Roslavl Forest, the Monastery's library received

---

* The Elder had been trying for twenty years, if not more, to buy certain volumes of the magazine *Christian Reading* which were missing in his collection and could not be found at bookstores; and only a year before his repose he received them as a consolatory gift from a pious person in Moscow, who donated those volumes to him from her library.

after Fr. Anthony's repose nearly sixty manuscripts of patristic works, Lives of Saints, and several outstanding collections of different rare prayers and church services. These manuscripts, none of which have ever been found among our printed books, were carefully collected by him and hand-copied in the pre-scribed manner.

Fr. Anthony had about *forty* handwritten and printed akathists, and he read each of them at least once a year, on the feast of that particular saint or on the feast day connected with the akathist. Fr. Anthony did not read any akathists which seemed in some way suspicious. Only once, while he was still living in the Skete, he received from somewhere a Uniate* collection of akathists and, unaware of the source, started read-ing the akathists out of his usual great zeal for the saints. While reading, he suddenly felt that the prayer somehow did not touch his heart or arouse any compunction, but that, on the contrary, there was something repulsive in it. He soon learned that it was not an Orthodox collection of akathists, and stopped reading them. Afterwards he became very strict and discriminating in his choice of them.

Once, a lady brought to the Elder of the Skete, Fr. Leonid, a service and akathist to God the Father, and asked him to review the manuscript to see if it was written according to the standard form. It had a beautiful cover and gilded edge. Fr. Leonid gave it for examination to Fr. Anthony, who said that since the Church did not adopt a separate service to God the Father, he

---

* Following the Union of Brest-Litovsk in 1596, the Roman church lured Orthodox bishops and laymen living in the Polish-Lithuanian Kingdom into union with Rome by allowing them to keep their beliefs and practices with the stipulation that they be in communion with the Pope at Rome. An individual member of this Union is sometimes called a "Uniate," and the ecclesiastical organization is thus called the Uniate Church. In this instance, the collection of akathists would allow room for non-Orthodox spirituality.

considered it to be dangerous to accept it. Fr. Leonid then said, "Well, then, give it here; we'll put it in the stove." Fr. Anthony objected: "But what will the lady say?" "Let her say what she wants; we won't pay any attention to her," the Elder said and burned the book.

After Fr. Anthony's repose, there was found in his cell a multitude of lists from different years of books which he had been planning to buy. There were also catalogs of books which he had collected, as well as various excerpts and remarks which indicated how much the Elder intended to enlarge his library and with what attention he read the books which he collected. Since the Lord had granted him an excellent memory,* the Elder by steady and attentive reading enriched and developed his mind. He surprised those with whom he conversed by his broad, comprehensive education and by the resourcefulness with which he could often suddenly cite in his conversations what he had read. His citations were always to the point of the subject at hand. Listening to his conversation one could not imagine that Fr. Anthony had not even attended a public school, but had learned to read and write from the Psalter and Horologion at home.

Fr. Anthony's inquisitiveness was always directed toward spiritual profit. He liked to read, but even more he liked to fulfill what he read. His inquisitiveness was penetrated by and applied through the spirit of asceticism in such a way that the words of the educated and humble Elder never in the least sounded like the usual book-knowledge. All his words were

---

* The Elder himself said that he remembered everything he read during the last five years. He was able to tell exactly day by day what happened, who visited him, and about what they spoke—everything to the minutest detail; and more important matters remained clearly and indelibly preserved in his memory since his childhood. He could remember with amazing detail things he had read even during the last thirty years.

directed toward spiritual benefit, being a product of his active mind.

As a great lover of silence, Fr. Anthony had always wished to spend a solitary life in prayerful labors, reading, and meditation upon God. He used to say that when he was alone in his cell, it seemed a feast day to his soul. Out of his great humility he always avoided instructing others because in Optina Monastery there was already a great Elder, Hieromonk Macarius, who was greatly respected by everyone and was appointed by the blessed Elder, Fr. Leonid, to spiritually guide all who hastened to him.

The firm wish of Fr. Anthony was to be considered no more than another monk living in retirement in the Monastery. Yet his spiritual gifts, and even his own humility by which he avoided all, attracted everyone to him; and soon his cell was filled with a multitude of visitors wishing to receive his blessing and spiritual edification. According to the words of our Saviour Himself: *Him that cometh to Me I will in no wise cast out* (John 6:37). Out of love for his neighbors, the Elder could not avoid participating in the lives of the people who visited him. However, with profound wisdom he did not exceed the limits of his humble position. He refused to listen to confessions and sent everyone to the monastery confessors. Only in very rare, extraordinary cases could he be persuaded to make an exception to this rule. He accepted only a few people for continual spiritual guidance, chiefly those who had come to him in Maloyaroslavets or previously, when he was the Superior in the Skete. Others he spiritually aided without taking upon himself the responsibility or the attitude of a spiritual instructor or guide.

It seemed that his chief and only worry was how to be friendly and to offer everyone gracious hospitality and respect. Fr. Anthony showed boundless respect to all; he humbled himself very courageously before everyone and was not afraid to

Elder Macarius
† 1860

humiliate himself by doing so. He was not ashamed to show such a degree of respect to a youth, or even to a child, which people of another background would not show even to their elders. In this Fr. Anthony could not be excelled.

One novice revealed his thoughts to him: "When I meet someone younger than I, I can't, without first making an effort, bow down before him, especially if the person whom I have met doesn't respond to me with a bow in return, for then I feel sort of ashamed." "This happens in the beginning from worldly habits," answered Fr. Anthony, "but now I could prostrate myself at the feet of anyone, even a beggar, right in the middle of Red Square in Moscow, and I wouldn't be embarrassed at all."

With sincerity of heart, Fr. Anthony humbled himself limitlessly before everyone. Everyone felt that his inner humility and benevolence to all were really sincere and not a mere display. His heart was always full of sympathy for his sorrowing neighbors, and therefore he especially liked to comfort those who came to him.

In his youth, due to his exalted spiritual thoughts and his leading of a strict life, he was strict also in regard to others, and he involuntarily became upset and ashamed of the faults of his weaker brethren. But the wise admonitions of his older brother Fr. Moses and his own progress in the spiritual life later brought Fr. Anthony to such a state of mind that, although being very strict with himself, he at the same time had a fatherly condescension towards the faults of others and in some cases made allowances for them.

He never despaired of anyone's correction and knew how to inspire slothful and fainthearted people. No matter how despondent someone might be, he always succeeded by his counsels in inspiring that person with hope. Fr. Anthony was very careful in giving advice and admonitions, being guided by the teaching of St. Isaac the Syrian, who said that such people should be treated as infirm and be comforted rather than accused; accusations would make them more upset and would not bring about any benefit. The Elder said, "One should say to one who is sick, 'Would you care for some soup or something else?' rather than saying, 'I will give you a drug which will really open your eyes!'" Fr. Anthony knew how to make people aware of their spiritual infirmities in such a way that they would not even notice. Once a person confessed before him some of his sins, but kept silent about some others. Fr. Anthony did not tell him that his confession was not complete; on the contrary, he told him that by his confession he made the angels in heaven rejoice, and these words aroused in him contrition and eagerness to cleanse his conscience completely.

He never tried to convince anyone who did not want to listen to him, and his admonitions did not sound like commandments, but rather like hints or friendly advice. If someone tried to contradict him, he immediately stopped talking. He almost never gave straight answers to the questions of his visitors and even avoided questions which would clearly place him in the position of a teacher. Nevertheless, he skillfully directed general conversation in such a way that in talking about someone else or saying something about himself, he indirectly admonished and instructed those with whom he spoke. It happened often that upon leaving the Elder, a visitor would remember and understand that a remark made during the course of the conversation dealt directly with his concealed perplexities and faults, and this answered the questions which the Elder had not let him ask. To another, such a remark revealed something which he had not noticed before in himself. If someone inappropriately declared that he understood the Elder's idea and intention in such a remark, the Elder would immediately change the subject and start talking about ordinary matters. In general, the Elder was afraid to show his spiritual gifts and talked about strictly spiritual matters only with a few people. He also had great experience and wisdom in choosing how and to whom he should speak.

It was the general rule of Fr. Anthony, as well as of the other Elders, not to give advice to anyone without being asked for it, considering it to be not only useless, but also harmful idle talk. At the same time, Fr. Anthony watched with a vigilant eye those who were asking questions. If someone asked a question not out of spiritual need but from curiosity or for a similar reason, he did not answer at all.

Fr. Anthony used to say: "When someone asks a question, he receives profit from the answer according to his faith. If his faith is weak, he receives little benefit; if his faith is strong, he obtains great benefit. In the beginning I also would question the Elder, as if to test him, 'What will he say to that?' and I would receive the answers I deserved. But if someone believed in his heart that he would hear from the Elder the answer of God Himself, then God would give the answer, and the person would be transformed and would hear what he had not expected to hear."

In regard to some people, Fr. Anthony would only hint at their situation, but to simple people who received his words with simplicity of heart and with faith, he spoke plainly and simply. If someone had already proved throughout the many years of their spiritual relationship his sincerity and devotion, sometimes the Elder even called him to account.

It happened sometimes that one of his spiritual children would reveal to him a thought which bothered him, not in the course of confession, but in a simple conversation. The Elder would then mention it to him again and was satisfied only when everything had been confessed properly. He used to say in

Elder Hilarion
† 1873

conclusion, "Now everything is fine; otherwise you would have shown only the shell but not the nut itself."

He reminded several people who came to him of incidents which they not only had never revealed to him, but about which they had even forgotten. He would remind them to pray about one of their sins of which they were unaware, which they did not understand at all or did not consider to be a sin. Only much later, attentively examining their whole life, would they discover in themselves with amazement what the Elder had pointed out. The Elder would deal this way only with those people whose sincerity had been proven, and when it was clear to him that they kept things from him not out of stubbornness or lack of forthrightness, but only out of ignorance. However, in other cases, Fr. Anthony waited with extraordinary patience until the person would come to feel and realize this himself; only then could spiritual healing be effective. Likewise, if remarks made by him out of fatherly love and care were for some reason not received in the right way, he refrained from such remarks. Those whom he could not reach by his words, he tried secretly to direct to that which is profitable by his prayers.

Fr. Anthony had a natural gift of eloquence and even of mellifluous speech, and his words were always full of spiritual salt. Even when something was said in the form of a joke, it always contained exalted teaching and was exactly to the point, while at the same time being full of picturesque expressions.* Everyone felt that in Fr. Anthony's eloquence some great spiritual power was hidden. This power consisted, of course, in his teaching not from books but from deeds. All of his words were

---

* As he was born and raised in the Yaroslavl Province, Fr. Anthony did not want to change even with time his local Yaroslavl pronunciation (with stressed o's). This peculiarity sounded very agreeable in the speech of the simple Elder and embellished his conversation, so that even his Russian speech contained a trace of Church Slavonic dialect.

inspired by sincere kindness to those who questioned him, and were always preceded and followed by his zealous prayers for them to the Lord.

After becoming acquainted with someone, the Elder sometimes seemed to observe him for a while; in the beginning he spoke little and would only pray for him. But when he finally started talking, his words had such an irresistible power that sometimes during only a single conversation a person was spiritually reborn. People with an iron will and an inflexible character felt their stubbornness collapse, and their hearts were filled with new feelings. While they had never before yielded to anyone in anything, in listening to Fr. Anthony they conceived a strong desire never again to follow their own will and reason, but to submit their entire will to the holy Elder. Under the spiritual influence of Fr. Anthony and because of his fatherly care, people who had been carried away by liberalism and worldly life became sincere, zealous, and obedient children of the Holy Church; those who had surrendered to vanity and had been accustomed to having their whims fulfilled, devoted their lives to the humble monastic life; people who had been lost in the eyes of society and in their own eyes returned to the Christian life, renouncing the world and devoting the rest of their days to the Lord. Many people felt the spiritual power of Fr. Anthony, first being attracted to him by his love and condescension, and later imperceptibly coming to surrender their lives completely into his hands.

Fr. Anthony knew how to balance and combine fatherly condescension towards human weaknesses with a reasonable amount of strictness. First of all, he was inexorably strict in everything that concerned the teaching, tradition, and precepts of the Orthodox Church and, in general, all spiritual matters. If someone deviated from the strictness of the Church's norms, although Fr. Anthony avoided judging him, he could never agree with anything that contradicted the teaching of the Church in all its purity and strictness. No one could convince him to bless departure from the canonical rules. In such cases he kept repeating the words: "We are given the power to absolve sins, but not to absolve one to sin." Firmly believing in the teaching of the Church and unfailingly keeping Her precepts, he required of all his spiritual children the same undoubting faith and the same obedience. If someone contradicted him, he kept silent or avoided arguing, answering all objections with the same words, "So the Church teaches us; this has been handed down to us by the Holy Church." Secondly, since he personally set a perfect example of complete obedience to his elders, he strictly required from those who came to him the same behavior and respect for one's parents, authorities, and spiritual fathers, saying that these words of the Lord applied to them: *He that heareth you heareth Me* (Luke 10:16).

Finally, from those who were completely under his direction, he also required total obedience. Once he said something, he did not like to change or even repeat his words, often quoting the words of St. Gregory the Theologian, "Do we not consider one who stumbleth twice over the same stone senseless?" If one of his spiritual children, after receiving a command, asked the Elder about it again, he would not receive an answer.* There was no more severe punishment for his spiritual children than when the Elder said, "As you please." If while he was saying this his usually kind face became strict, none of them could bear to

---

* This feature had been present in his character since childhood. When he was fourteen, he was entrusted with teaching his little niece how to read and write. Once his mother, hearing the instruction suddenly stop, entered the room and found the teacher frowning and the student in tears. To her question about the reason for her tears, the little one replied that she did not know something and that her uncle had not told it to her. "I told her," he retorted.

see it without becoming very upset. In general, if someone disregarded a direction he had given, the Elder knew how to make him feel his guilt; and then, after tearful, sincere repentance, he would forgive him and become kind and loving again. However, he only treated his devoted spiritual children this way. In other cases, if he noticed that someone distrusted his words, then he knew how to withdraw, imperceptibly leaving him to carry the heavy burden of his own will. Even in such cases, however, he did not deprive him of his love and benevolence or even of his good opinion of him, trying inwardly to justify him.

One thing the Elder could not bear with indifference was grumbling, especially without good cause. He used to say that according to the words of St. Isaac the Syrian, even God Himself bears with all the weaknesses of men, but He will not suffer to leave without chastisement a man who murmurs continually.* Talking to such people, the kind Elder sometimes used sharp expressions, for which he was later ready to ask his spiritual children for their "gracious forgiveness and pardon." In general, if he noticed in someone's heart hostility against him, Fr. Anthony did not justify himself, but often asked forgiveness, stating that although his conscience did not accuse himself of anything, there is no man that lives and does not sin; God alone is without sin. He would also state what the holy Apostle Paul said about himself: *For of nothing against myself am I conscious, yet am I not hereby justified: but he that judgeth me is the Lord* (I Cor. 4:4).

Fr. Anthony received many letters from his spiritual children and acquaintances and, in spite of his many illnesses, compelled himself to answer the greater part of them in his

---

* Homily 85 in the Russian edition; Homily 48 in the English edition. (*The Ascetical Homilies of St. Isaac the Syrian*, Brookline, Massachusetts, Holy Transfiguration Monastery, 1984, p. 229.)

own hand. After his repose many letters were found, more than the people who had known him well had expected. Some letters containing general admonitions were chosen and published in a separate book. They are distinguished by the same dignity as his conversation, by the same natural eloquence and mellifluousness, and by the same edification, uniqueness of expression and power. Their style is totally unique and in harmony with Fr. Anthony's character. In them are clearly engraved all the great qualities of the loving Elder. In reading them one feels as if he were actually listening to the Elder's conversation. For this reason, we advise those who want to obtain a more complete understanding of Fr. Anthony to read his own letters, which will supplement the insufficiency of our sketch. In addition, we are going to add several examples of his letters which illustrate the power of Fr. Anthony's admonitions and his spiritual gifts.

Once, someone who was deeply grieved came to see Fr. Anthony because his only son, on whom he had placed all hope, had been expelled from school. "Do you pray for your son?" the Elder unexpectedly asked. "Sometimes I do," stammered the father, "but sometimes I don't." "Pray without fail for your son, pray fervently for him; the power of a parent's prayers for his children is great." After hearing these words, the inconsolable father, who until then had not been too diligent in prayer and in going to church, began to pray to the Lord for his son with all his soul. And what happened? After some time circumstances changed. The boy was again enrolled and finished his education with good grades, to the great consolation of his father. In the course of his entire life, his father had received only this one counsel from Fr. Anthony; yet he always remembered and spoke of him with tender feeling, saying that that one simple word of the divinely-wise Elder had brought great spiritual benefit to his whole life.

Two landowners once visited the Elder, and one of them was a "free-thinker." During the conversation he expressed doubt as to the truthfulness of the account about St. John, Archbishop of Novgorod, riding to Jerusalem for Pascha on a demon (Menology for the 7th of September). "One cannot believe such things." "Oh yes," answered the Elder instructively, "previously, the saints used to ride on demons, but now demons ride on various Russian aristocrats." And he laughed sadly with reproach. For some reason, these words produced such an impression on his listener that he suddenly fell silent, became embarrassed, and then cried. His friend immediately walked out of the room, leaving them alone. The topic and remainder of the conversation between the Elder and that man remain unknown, but the tears in the eyes of the visitor, who had before talked so freely, showed that his heart responded to the Elder's words; and although the free-thinking man tried afterwards to put on his usual airs, there were tears in his eyes for over an hour.

Someone expressed doubts about the testimony of Barsky, who wrote of his pilgrimage to the Holy Land, that in Jerusalem at Pascha the blessed fire descends from heaven. "If you saw it yourself, would you believe?" asked Fr. Anthony. "I would." "Well, who should we believe more, you who didn't see it or Barsky who did?"

A young girl, saying good-bye to the Elder, jokingly asked him to pray that the Lord would help her to get married. "But you really don't want to get married," the Elder said to her. "Yes, I do," she insisted. After some time, when she again visited Fr. Anthony he met her with these words, "Why are you deceiving me? I was even going to write you." When the girl—who had already forgotten about her joke which she, by worldly understanding, considered quite innocent (even while talking to a spiritual man)—answered in perplexity that she did not remember having fooled him, Fr. Anthony reminded her that upon leaving she had asked him to pray for her. "Remembering your wish, three times I started praying for you and three times I heard a voice saying, 'It is not what she needs.' So why did you deceive me?"

Another individual, when Fr. Anthony turned upon her his searching and penetrating glance, sincerely explained that she was afraid when he looked at her this way. "You see all my sins," she said. "You are wrong in thinking so," replied the Elder. "What I pray for and what God reveals to me, that I am able to know, but if God doesn't reveal something to me, then I don't know anything."

Once a worried clerk came to Fr. Anthony with a request, "Father, tomorrow I am going to fight a duel. Please serve a moleben asking God to protect me." "What?! What are you talking about?" replied the Elder. "You are going to fight a duel in order to kill a man and you ask help from God? Don't you realize what you have said? The sixth commandment says: 'Thou shalt not kill.' Even civil law prohibits duels, and you have come to me, a servant of the altar, asking me to bless you to fight a duel in order to commit murder! We pray for peace, for the forgiveness of offenses. I ask you to abandon this ungodly deed and humble yourself. If you have been insulted, forgive; and if you have insulted someone, ask forgiveness. If you wish, I am ready to ask forgiveness for you." And so with the help of God this matter was settled peacefully.

The following are memoirs from people who knew Abbot Anthony well:

"Soon after entering Optina Monastery," I. A. writes, "since my Elder Fr. Macarius was absent, with the blessing of Archimandrite Moses I started to go for revelation of thoughts to Abbot Anthony. I wanted to take advantage of my relationship as his disciple and wanted at once to reveal my entire life to him, or at least the most important parts of it. Usually, upon approaching him I knelt, and in such a position confided my thoughts and received admonition. But when I arrived to reveal my entire life to him, having barely opened the door, he came to me hastily, and I bent over in order to kneel; but he lifted me up and hurriedly said, 'No, please, don't kneel, don't kneel, please. The Elder himself will soon return (that is, Fr. Macarius, whom he humbly called the Elder). Explain everything to him, explain it to him; he will come back soon. Goodbye!' In this way he not only did not let me confess before him the history of my entire life, but did not even listen to my usual revelation of thoughts, although he had readily listened to it every day previously. I left without anything."

"One evening," as one novice who was a secretary for Fr. Anthony told us, "I found Fr. Anthony changing bandages on his afflicted legs, at which sight even a stranger couldn't look without shuddering. Feeling sympathy for the Elder because of his sufferings, my heart grew warm with love for him and I thought to myself, 'The Elder doesn't even know or suppose that I love him with all my heart.' As soon as I had this thought, he said to me, 'I'm well aware that P. P. loves me very much,' and he asked me, 'Is it true what I have said?' I answered him in this way, 'Father, you have spoken the truth that I dearly love you with all my heart.'"

The same novice writes, "Once I imprudently told one of the fathers in the Monastery of an incident which testified to the Elder's clairvoyance. A short time later Fr. Anthony sent his cell-attendant to ask me to come to him. Upon my arrival, I saw the Elder coming out of his door in a very troubled state. His face was pale and expressed great agitation and anger. He said, 'Here is what I want to tell you: if you want to profit from my counsel, I ask you not to reveal to anyone my words and conversations with you; treasure them only in your own heart.' Wishing to calm the Elder, I promised to fulfill his command exactly. Blessing me, he dismissed me."

"Many times," wrote novice A. of D. Convent, "I happened to speak with Fr. Anthony, but I liked especially to listen when he would tell about his life in the desert. Father himself liked to reminisce about it, always saying that he never felt as well and content as he did in the desert. Yet, the hermits' life was very poor. They lived in a forest not having anything, though they had spent their youth living with their families in near luxury. 'Sometimes,' Father said, 'while I was still asleep, mother would be calling, "Get up, breakfast is ready," and then different pleasures would follow one after another.' But there in the desert they ate only vegetables from the garden, or rather only turnips because nothing else grew there. It was very seldom that some landowner would send them bread. This they treasured like *prosphora,* so that not a crumb of it would be dropped. Once, the Elder related, they had so little food for Pascha that there was almost nothing to eat. But they did not despair. They sang Matins and with such icons as they had went in procession around the cell singing the joyful 'Christ is risen,' being comforted in soul and rejoicing in the Lord. When the time came for the *trapeza* (meal), Fr. Moses poured some oil from an icon lamp into the turnip soup and blessed them to break the fast. But the Lord only wanted thereby to test their patience, because on the very next day a neighboring landowner sent them provisions.

"O wondrous Elder! Who can describe all the love which he felt for his neighbors? How was he able to know how to console everyone who came to him with any sort of grief? No matter what lay upon one's soul, all flew away at his words. It even seemed that stepping over the threshold of his cell and looking at his holy face could make one forget everything. He himself knew what to say to whom and with what to console his visitor, because he had the gift of clairvoyance.

"Once I came to him because I was perplexed by several thoughts and also felt some sadness in my heart. I did not explain it to the Elder, for we were not alone. Saying farewell to all of us, the Elder put his hand on my shoulder and said, 'Don't be sad! God's Providence will arrange everything for the best; trust in Him.' And everything flew away; I felt an ineffable peaceful spirit without even confiding to him what I wanted. It seemed that the Elder himself came to know what was on my mind.

"Another time I was again surprised at his clairvoyance. I visited him with my brother and sister. The conversation began and continued about different matters which didn't interest me. I first silently murmured at my brother because he talked to the Elder about such empty things and only tormented the sick Elder; but, seeing that Batiushka didn't change the subject, I dared to grumble at the Elder himself. 'What is this,' I thought. 'Father knows that we came for a short time; why doesn't he say something for our souls' benefit? What is the use of this conversation?' When we were saying goodby to the Elder, he blessed everyone, but when I came and bowed to him, he said, 'You must forgive me for talking about unnecessary things.' I was very startled at these words, but he added kindly, 'Come to me after Vespers.' Yes, there were many cases indicating his clairvoyance. Sometimes someone wanted to ask about a subject but didn't know how, and the Elder himself would start to talk about it and would give direct answers to the questions he hadn't asked."

Finally, we offer to our readers the notes about Abbot Anthony written by Simeon Ivanovich Yanovsky,* the former

---

* See Yanovsky's Life: Abbot Herman, "Schemamonk Sergius Yanovsky, An Around the World Adventure into Sanctity," *The Orthodox Word* (St. Herman Brotherhood, 1990), Vol. 26, nos. 1-2, pp. 4-108.

principal of Kaluga Junior College. He was an esteemed and seasoned eighty-year-old veteran who, with the old, primitively equipped Russian navy, twice sailed around the world. He lived for several years in the North American Colonies with the well-known A. A. Baranov,* and after going through all these worldly vicissitudes is now peacefully spending the rest of his life in a monastery. The opinion of such an experienced old gentleman has a special value and meaning.

"When I went into retirement," he said, "there was no house on our estate, and we had to live in Kaluga in a rented apartment. Although we lived very modestly, we didn't have enough money to support our large family on the income from our estate and my pension, and so we were running into debt. For that reason it became necessary to build a house in the village. Therefore I turned to Fr. Anthony with the request: 'Batiushka, bless me to build a house in the village.' 'May it be so,' he answered. 'May God bless you!' 'I am also asking you to pray for God's help.' 'I will pray.' I have to mention that at that time we had only 400 roubles in banknotes and 100 prepared logs for building. With such poor means I started building a rather large house. And what happened? Through the prayers and blessing of Fr. Anthony, God, beyond our expectations, sent us so much help that within one summer the house was roughly built and covered. The next summer, floors were laid and stoves, window frames, and doors were installed. Towards autumn we were already able to move in and live there. When we counted everything, the house alone, without further additions, cost us more than 2,000 silver roubles, and with the service buildings more than 3,000 roubles. The house was warm, peaceful, spacious, and beautiful. It was obvious that the Lord helped us through Fr. Anthony's prayers and blessings.

* *Ibid.,* pp. 17-32.

Schemamonk Sergius Yanovsky, a disciple of
Saints Herman of Alaska and Anthony of Optina.

"In 1860, before Cheesefare Sunday I caught a cold and became very ill while living in the country. A carbuncle appeared on my spine. I went to Confession and received Holy Communion. They brought a doctor from Kaluga who examined me and said that I should be taken to Kaluga immediately. I suffered terribly on my trip because of the bumps in the road, but, thanks be to God, I arrived there. At the same time our neighbor was going to Optina for Confession and Holy Communion. I asked her to tell the Optina Elders about my sickness and also to ask Fr. Moses, Fr. Macarius, and Fr. Anthony to pray for my recovery. All of them were very concerned about me, and Fr. Anthony firmly said, 'His family must pray, too. God is merciful; He will recover.' And really, God heard his prayers. I was over seventy years old and was so gravely ill that the doctors had little hope. They operated on me and the Lord, through the prayers of the venerable Fr. Anthony and through the tearful entreaties of my family, healed me—one can even say, resurrected me from my deathbed.

"In 1863, we decided to go on pilgrimage to Zadonsk and Voronezh. At that time it wasn't safe to travel. Towns and villages were being burned down; there were many robberies, and even landowners' homes were plundered. Not far away from us a large merchants' settlement and several villages had burned down. It was dangerous to leave the estate and the house. I wrote to Fr. Anthony: 'Father, bless us! We intend to go on pilgrimage to St. Tikhon and to Voronezh. Pray for God's help and our safe journey. Since this is such a dangerous time—there are so many robberies, and towns and villages are being burned down—what do you advise us to do? Should we all leave the house and our estate, or should one of us stay back (myself, of course)?' He answered, 'All of you go. It is said, *The angel of the Lord will encamp round about them that fear Him* (Psalm 33:7). Leave behind a reliable man; entrust everything to God, and all of you should go. God is merciful; everything will be safe and will turn out well.' So, relying on his prayers, we all went on the trip: me, my wife, and our four daughters in our coach with four horses. With us was also a hired coachman who sometimes drank like a fish. After praying to God, we left the village on the 2nd of September. In this autumn month rain and mud could be expected on the roads, but we, through the prayers of Fr. Anthony, had beautiful, dry weather the entire time. It was warm and nice, better than in summer because it was not too hot. So our trip went beautifully, and we all went on the pilgrimage and returned in good health. None of the horses grew weak, the coach rode smoothly, the coachman stayed sober and behaved well, and at home we found everything safe and in order. This is how powerful Fr. Anthony's prayer was!

"Once I went with my daughter and my son to Optina Monastery to prepare ourselves to receive Holy Communion. We spent the Feast of the Annunciation there. The winter roads had already started to become muddy and the river swelled considerably. On the day of the Annunciation, after Liturgy we went to Fr. Anthony, said farewell and received his blessing for travelling. After lunch, we harnessed the horses to the carriage and packed our things. An awful snowstorm started and, as the saying goes, one couldn't see the light of God: it was impossible to travel. This upset me very much, and I felt depressed and sad. I went into a separate room, knelt in front of an icon, and prayed with tears saying, 'O Lord! I am not worthy to be heard by Thee; but through the prayers of Thy slave, Fr. Anthony, stop this blizzard and make it possible for us to travel.' And what happened? To my great astonishment and joy, the snow started falling more softly and, just as I arose after my prayer, the blizzard stopped and we left immediately. Soon the sun came out, and we safely reached Kaluga and came to our village.

"While inspecting the schools, one night I was travelling from Ludin's factory to the main road on my way to the village of Maklaka. An awful blizzard began and it became very cold. I wasn't familiar with that locality, and we lost our way and wandered around. We couldn't find any dwelling or road and became desperate, being in danger of freezing to death. I silently prayed to God to deliver us from danger and show us the way, through the prayers of His slave, Fr. Anthony. Suddenly, two people appeared. I asked them to show us the way to Maklaka village and promised them a reward. One of them went with the coachman, while the other walked along with the coach, and we started moving slowly. During the entire time the latter was observing what was inside the coach. Next to me lay a loaded musket and a sabre, and I took the musket in my hand. We travelled this way for an hour. Suddenly, they turned the horses in a different direction. I ordered the coachman to sit down and turn the coach so that the wind would be blowing from the right side. Then those who were accompanying us left us and ran away. Later on, we found out that they were robbers. Soon we heard the barking of dogs and came to the fence of the village of Maklaka. Thanks be to God, we arrived safely at an inn and spent the night there. There we learned that before our arrival, the robbers had been in the village and had plundered a house. That is how the Lord, through the prayers of Fr. Anthony, sent the robbers to show us the way. Many similar things happened to me. Many times at night I lost my way, prayed silently to the Lord to show me the way through the prayers of Fr. Anthony, and immediately help came—either a passerby, a wagon, or a sled appeared and showed me the road.

"Once we sent a man to Kaluga from our village to do some shopping for us and bring our mail, the newspaper, and fifty silver roubles. This was in autumn. The next evening the man was expected to return, but towards evening there was rain and wind. It became very dark; the roads were treacherous and bridges were poor. The man had not yet returned, and I was very worried. The clock struck eight o'clock, then nine o'clock. The rain increased, the horse was weakening, and the man was not entirely reliable. It was eleven o'clock and everyone went to bed. I started to pray with tears, asking the merciful God to bring the man home safely through the prayers of Fr. Anthony. Would you believe it? I assure you upon my honor, I was making my third prostration when I heard the entrance door open. I took a candle and went there. What joy and surprise! The man, all soaked, had returned safely and brought everything I had asked for. My eyes were filled with tears of gratitude. There were many cases in my life when I quickly received help through the prayers of Fr. Anthony.

"My daughter, the young maiden E.,* had been sick for quite a long time. She caught a cold and coughed; drugs didn't help. She lost much weight, could barely walk, and was beginning to contract consumption. We asked Fr. Anthony to pray for her. He promised he would, and at that time she visibly started to recover. God resurrected her and she recovered completely and is now in good health.

"Here is another case. We were living in the village very quietly, almost in solitude, but we still were often in a poor and difficult situation. Once I was very sad and became so depressed because of many debts and also because of slander (even from my close ones) that deep sorrow befell me. Suddenly I received an unexpected letter from the venerable Fr. Anthony, who wrote, 'Read such and such a Life, and the Lord will console you.' This surprised me very much. How could he, being sixty-five miles away, know about my grief and the reason for

---

* Yanovsky's daughter Elizabeth, who painted the first portrait of St. Herman of Alaska from her father's description.

my sadness? This very Life was directly related to my sorrow and the circumstances I was in, and I was truly consoled and pacified. Having read it, I gained great hope in God's help. Console him there, O Lord, in the future life, in the same way as he consoled me in this life.

"How hospitable and kind he was! When we came to Optina and visited him, he used to treat us to tea. He would sometimes serve it himself despite his sickness and would invite us to eat as well, treating us to everything that he had received as gifts. He didn't eat, he only treated others. He poured honey mead into glasses from a bottle and offered it to us saying, 'Drink, please. This drink is cold but is served from a heart made warm by love.' Truly, what a delicious, pleasant drink this was, and so was the tea served with his blessing!

"When three of my daughters decided to enter a convent, they asked Fr. Anthony to ask on their behalf for my consent. When he conveyed to me my daughters' wish, I was somewhat troubled. I said, 'Father, what are my wife and I going to do without any help in our old age?' He replied, 'You will still have one daughter and a son.' I argued, saying that my financial means were severely limited, and I couldn't give them more than two hundred silver roubles annually for their support and that would be insufficient. He said, 'Don't worry about that, God will send help; only good will is necessary.' And truly his words were fulfilled. With God's invisible help everything was arranged. Soon we had the opportunity to buy a spacious, comfortable, and almost new cell for my daughters. When they were allowed to wear the monastic habit which had to be sewn at their own expense, a deposit was also required and we did not have any money. We were in a difficult financial situation. Long ago I had offered for sale my entire estate and a small separate plot of empty land consisting of sixty acres, but not a single buyer had appeared. Now to our great

Abbess Angelina Yanovsky, daughter of Sergius I. Yanovsky
and spiritual daughter of Abbot Anthony.

surprise, through the prayers of Fr. Anthony some people came to Kaluga from the Tula Province eighty-five miles away in order to buy this small, empty lot. The ad in the newspapers read, 'Please contact our son in Kaluga. His name is so and so.' But just at that time our son went on business to the provinces of Ryazan and Voronezh. Consequently, this lady, since she would not have been able to find our son at home, would have returned home and the bargain would not have taken place. But by God's Providence it happened that my wife and I went to Kaluga in order to have a moleben served and to venerate the wonder-working Kaluga icon of the Mother of God, which had been brought to Kaluga at that time. It was a wondrous thing that we and the potential buyer came to Kaluga on the same day. The next day she came to us with an offer. I took her to the empty plot of land. She liked it—even the incline and the location of the land were in complete conformity with her desire. We concluded the business immediately. The buyer offered almost the same price which I had requested. In this way, we made the deposit for our daughters in the convent, bought the habits for them, and also used part of the money for some other needs. How fortunate they are now that the Lord has delivered them from the world, and, moreover, that He has not abandoned them!

"Through the prayers of Fr. Anthony we have conveniently and peacefully settled up the accounts with our peasants and they are provided for. Through his prayers we finally sold our estate and were able to pay off all our large debts to the extent of 15,000 roubles, and there was enough money left for our children. I was very happy that I had paid back all my debts and could die peacefully, not owing anything to anyone. It should be mentioned that our estate had been advertised for sale long before for 20,000 roubles, but no one had made an offer. Finally, a buyer offered 18,000, half of it down in bank notes and part on credit. We would lose 2,000 roubles, and it was not to our advantage; I nevertheless agreed, but the customer withdrew his offer. I told Fr. Anthony about the sale of the estate. He said to me: 'Lower the price a little, and if someone offers 15,000 silver roubles cash, not on credit, then agree and sell it.' I said, 'All right, it is cheap, but we have to sell it.' It happened that on the very day of Fr. Anthony's repose, August 7th, a buyer appeared with whom we tried to negotiate at the higher price but did not succeed, and had to settle for 15,000 roubles, the very sum which Fr. Anthony had set.

"Once, before the Feast of Holy Pascha, I wrote to Abbot Anthony: 'Our neighbors A. and V., whom you know, are hopelessly ill. The first has been sick for two years from breast cancer; part of her flesh has even rotted away to such an extent that the bones are visible. The other one is also gravely ill; the doctors say there is no hope. She has seven little children. Please pray to God for them.' He answered that the first one would be cleansed of her sins through this sickness. She must be patient and not grumble. The second one would be spared by God for the sake of her children. In fact, the first one, after suffering, was granted a splendid Christian death. And the other one, in spite of the doctors' prognosis, started to recover; and, strangely enough, her health started to improve on the very day that Fr. Anthony wrote the letter. She recovered and was able to walk about. But right now she is sick again. It's obvious that this is pleasing to the Lord God and must be so.

"Through the blessing and prayers of Fr. Anthony, the Lord brought me for a life of repentance to a holy monastery.* Many incidents prove that Fr. Anthony had the gift of clairvoyance. It happened several times that I had the intention of telling him

* St. Tikhon of Kaluga Monastery.

about something and asking his advice, but he read my thoughts and forestalled me, saying, 'You want to do this or want to ask me about that,' and would tell me straightway what I was thinking about and would give me counsel. When we were ready to leave for home and were saying farewell, he gave little gifts to all of us: a little icon, a candlestick, a little book or something else for remembrance. Then he blessed us and saw us off, even coming down from the porch and walking with us on his afflicted legs to the gate, blessing us constantly. Sometimes we saw tears in his eyes—such was his love for us!

"We visited him for the last time at the end of July when he was on his deathbed. On the first of August after the Divine Liturgy we said farewell forever. In spite of his grave sickness, he received us with great love and talked to us a little. He sat up on his bed, blessed every member of our family, remembered those who were absent and blessed them *in absentia*. To each one he gave a little icon. Finally, we parted from him in tears, and he cried too. Our angel, our benefactor! May he enter into the joy of his Lord! To the one God may there be glory forever! Amen!"

Finally, we would regard it as a sin to be silent about a remarkable incident in the life of Fr. Anthony. This incident clearly reveals the power of his prayers and also the nature of the attacks of the enemy of the human race on spiritual people because of their care for the salvation of others.

The devout maiden R. (now a novice in the T. Convent) was subjected to the same temptation as the holy Martyr Justina: she was pursued by a certain man who, seeing that he could not seduce her in spite of all his efforts, turned to a sorcerer and, with his help, cast a spell on the girl. Being warned about this through a faithful servant-woman and beginning to feel the effects of the enemy's power, this maiden had no one to seek help from except God. She had no acquaintance with anyone of spiritual life. One night the servant-woman saw a dream wherein a tall monk entered her lady's room and led her out dressed in a monastic garment. Soon after this dream, the girl's relatives, who until then had never hosted any monks in their house, unexpectedly expressed their wish to meet Abbot Anthony. In the evening of the same day, by the special design of God's Providence, Fr. Anthony without any invitation visited that family although he had never met them before. This visit was very important, for by it was clearly indicated the Providence of God for this family, the manifest activity of the demons of which many folk are now unconscious, as well as the spiritual power of Fr. Anthony. Here is what we know for sure about this visit:

When Fr. Anthony entered the house, a large crowd of demons visibly attacked him with curses and threats, forbidding him entrance. The Elder was not frightened by the threats of the enemies of the human race; he humbly invoked the help of the Name of God, and God drove them away. When Fr. Anthony entered, everybody noticed that his face was deadly pale. The servant-woman, seeing him, recognized him as the man whom she had seen in her dream. The young maiden R. from her first glance felt complete spiritual openness and confidence towards Fr. Anthony, and decided to tell him the story of her entire life. The Elder understood that the only salvation for this maiden was to go to a convent, but her relatives did not even wish to hear of this. Fr. Anthony did not find it possible or profitable to persuade them, and therefore he only prayed for her deliverance from the enemy's nets which surrounded her. By his letters he strengthened her in her torment from the invisible power of demons which had been brought against her by the sorcerer. After a while, Fr. Anthony advised the entire family to visit N. Monastery, where several people were being tonsured into monasticism. This advice was accepted, and through Fr.

Anthony's prayers the rite of tonsure made such a deep impression on the mother of the maiden R. that when leaving the church she unexpectedly gave her consent for her daughter to enter the convent. The maiden R., with great joy and thanksgiving to God, made haste to take advantage of her mother's permission and entered the T. Convent where she now lives. However, the sorcerer boasted that he would drag her even out of the convent. And indeed the young novice continued to feel within herself the action of the enemy's power, having repose neither day nor night. Again she found strength in the prayers and counsels of Fr. Anthony. The young sufferer received final deliverance from the temptation of the enemy that tormented her through the prayers of the great hierarch, Metropolitan Philaret of Moscow, now reposed in the Lord, whose name is revered everywhere in Russia and even outside of Russia. Once, he appeared to the Maiden R. in a dream, read the 60th Psalm, ordered her to repeat after him all the verses of it, and then gave her the obedience to read this psalm daily. Upon awakening, she felt that the temptation which had been tormenting her for many years had completely departed from her.

We know that this account might appear unbelievable to many readers, but do we not find a multitude of similar cases in the narrations of the lives of the saints which the holy Church considers to be true? Furthermore, the reliability of this account, which was taken down from the maiden's own words, is confirmed by the very letters of Fr. Anthony to her, which we received and published in their original form in the collection of Abbot Anthony's letters under numbers 296-298*. Here are the actual words of Fr. Anthony from his letter of the 2nd of October, 1864:

---

* *Letters of Abbot Anthony to Various People* (Moscow: Optina Monastery, 1869), Letter 298 of the 2nd of October, 1864, pp. 380-1.

"When the hour arrived that I, by the will of God, came to visit you, I first encountered a whole crowd of demons. With abusive language they prohibited me from entering, but the Lord drove them away. Although I am myself a great sinner and not worthy to save others, the Lord God by His great mercy to you chose me, unworthy as I am, as an instrument to speedily lead you forth from the deep abyss (which was revealed beforehand in your servant's dream). If we would have postponed your departure for another year or more, then only God knows what else might have happened to you. Your experience during the last two years spent in your parents' home was revealed to me so clearly that I cannot think of it without a heartfelt shudder. Not knowing this beforehand, I was right in advising you to pray to the holy Virgin-Martyr Justina, for your situation then was very similar to hers, as I have just recently learned. With my whole heart I thank God with tears that your holy soul has been delivered from the nets which had ensnared it."

In conclusion, there is the story about a worthy disciple of Fr. Anthony who by God's Providence was sent as a consolation to the Elder for all his labors in the salvation of his neighbors. She also showed by her own example how powerful Fr. Anthony's influence was on his spiritual children and what fruits were manifest through his guidance when it was received with faith. From her youth, the young maiden of high society, Katherine Alexandrovna P., felt the Lord calling her to the spiritual life and deemed everything earthly as transitory and empty. However, she did not find any support for her disposition of soul. She unwillingly took part in the life and routines of the society in which she had been raised, and spent many years in Petersburg in light-minded society and in the "din of vanity," as Fr. Anthony later termed it.

Upon meeting the Elder, she submitted herself with burning faith to his spiritual guidance. Under his influence her good natural qualities were properly guided. The call of God to a life of godliness became stronger and prevailed over her short-lived delights in earthly vanity. Soon a decision to withdraw from the world and draw near to God through solitude, prayer, abstinence, and the strict preservation of chastity burned within her. Family ties did not allow Katherine Alexandrovna to break with the world completely, but she, amidst worldly vanity, lived a life of piety and found spiritual consolation in visiting Optina Monastery, where she stayed in the guesthouse. In short, it could be said of her that the disciple was like her Elder.

She was an example of zealous prayer and attendance at church services. When living in Petersburg, she had not gotten up earlier than 10:00 a.m., whereas now she was already dressed at 1:00 a.m, and as soon as the bell rang for Matins, she hurried to church in order to arrive there before the prayers began. In general, the chime of church bells calling for any service found her always ready to go to church or already on the way. Her spiritual relationship with the Elder grew, according to her own words, not by the day but by the hour. Finally she reached such a blessed state that she became a true novice of Elder Anthony. She concentrated only on the church of God and her Elder. Being concerned only about the salvation of her soul, she strove to fulfill all the Elder's commands without breaking any of them in the least manner. Nothing else for her existed.

Teaching her obedience, Fr. Anthony sometimes cut off some of her seemingly good desires. Thus, although it was the greatest consolation for K. A. to see the Elder and converse with him, Fr. Anthony at one time while she was at Optina blessed her to come to him only once a week; on the other days she was allowed to receive his blessing only in church. This was a most difficult and sensitive trial for Katherine Alexandrovna. Sometimes she could not control herself and sought an occasion to see the Elder on other days; she herself acknowledged that she was then deprived of peace of mind, being afflicted by sadness and boredom. However, when she fulfilled precisely the Elder's command, she felt in her soul delightful peace and quiet. Such is the power of obedience!

The Holy Fathers call the cutting off of one's own will the shortest path to salvation. Many doers of blessed obedience, such as St. Dositheus,* in a short time attained great spiritual heights, and thus completed their earthly course. So it was with K. A.; after four years of spiritual guidance under Abbot Anthony, she died when she was only thirty years old. Her blessed and extraordinary end proved to all what exalted heights can be reached in a short time by a person following the Gospel path of obedience to one's spiritual father. We offer here some excerpts from the notes of Fr. Anthony in which he describes the last days and edifying end of K. A.

"Beginning with spring and during the whole summer, K. A. burned and melted as a candle each day. That is, she was gradually losing her physical strength. Her favorite topic of conversation was the transition to eternity. She was preparing for her death each day in the way a bride prepares for her wedding crown, with a bright face and joyful heart. On July 27th, she received Holy Unction with the anointing of holy oil.** She would receive the Holy Mysteries of Christ every third day, or even every other day, and during the last week of her life, daily. After having received Holy Unction, she was brought to me every day, being supported by the arms; later she had to

---

* The disciple of St. Dorotheos of Gaza.

** A month prior to her death, in spite of her illness, K. A. expressed her wish to receive the Mystery of Unction in church. At the same time, she received the tonsure into the monastic habit in her cell.

be carried in a chair. I would also visit her in the guesthouse every day, or even two or three times a day.

"After K. A. was tonsured into the angelic habit, I congratulated her during visits and asked her, 'Sister, what is your name in the angelic rank?' She would answer, 'Very sinful nun Euphrosyne.' I would ask her next, 'What does your new name mean?' And she would reply, 'Joy and gladness.' To this I would say, 'May the Lord grant you eternal rejoicing and gladness with the saints in the Heavenly Kingdom!' And with a joyful countenance she always thanked me, 'Oh how grateful I am for this holy name!' This manner of questioning was repeated every day, according to her wish, until her death.

"From the day she received Holy Unction, she seemed to be reborn. Her heart breathed with love towards all; she pitied all. She asked forgiveness of those present and those absent, and became friendly with everyone. To her very death she was found to be in a prayerful state of soul; her prayer rope did not drop from her hand for a minute. In the last week of her life I asked her how she prayed. She answered me: 'This is how: "Lord have mercy, Lord have mercy, Lord have mercy! Most Holy Theotokos, Queen of Heaven, my Mother, take me to Thyself! Holy Archangel Michael, Holy Archangel Gabriel, Holy Archangel Raphael, receive my soul! St. Nicholas, great Saint of God, protect my soul!"' In a similar manner she invoked many other saints, asking them for help at the time of the departure of her soul. These truly childlike prayers especially touched me. Before her death she gave away all her belongings, saying, 'Coming into this world I had nothing, and leaving the world I don't wish to own anything.' After distributing everything she said joyfully, 'Now I have nothing at all apart from hope in God's salvation.' She sincerely wished to leave everything to me, but I, in order not to hurt her feelings, agreed to take only very little, and that I spent for the commemoration of her soul. Two weeks before her end, a coffin had been prepared for her; and two days before she died, she asked me to let her be carried alive into the church so that she might die there, but I refused to do this.

"The Canon for the Departure of the Soul was read over her eight or ten times, and she read the end of it by herself and said, 'My beloved fathers, brothers and sisters, and all whom I know! Remember my love and friendship, and pray to Christ the God of all to be merciful to me at the hour of my death and after my death.' In the meantime she confessed daily, and again mentally asked everyone for forgiveness. Every evening I sprinkled her with holy Theophany water and bid her farewell. She died on the Feast of the Beheading of the Honorable, Glorious Prophet, Forerunner and Baptist of the Lord, John, following the Vigil, right after midnight.* Half an hour before her death, she requested that the candles be lit in front of all the icons in her guesthouse cell and began to rejoice, saying, 'What gladness there is now in my soul, as if it were a feast day!' Soon she had inner spasms which abruptly stopped her breathing. Lying for three days in her coffin she didn't look dead, but looked like a sleeping virgin; and her face didn't change at all, except that she didn't speak. Having read the prayer of absolution, I placed this prayer in her hands and noticed that they were soft, not stiff. Truly wondrous is God not only in His saints, but also in the midst of us unworthy sinners! Revering the one who reposed in blessedness, although I have already written much about her, I cannot say enough about her last days.

"Now I visit her daily for an hour or more and delight in her sepulchre, which is much better than her cell when she lived

---

* Abbot Anthony at first felt sorry that K. A. had died at night and not during the day. But when he told this to Archimandrite Moses, the latter reassured and consoled him, saying, "What's the matter? Is it not said, *Behold, the Bridegroom cometh in the middle of the night*" (From the Midnight Service, also, cf. Matt. 25:6).

among us. It has two large, bright windows and is adorned with many icons. On the wall next to the coffin is depicted Christ's burial, an *epitaphion* before which a *lampada* burns continually. I pray for the reposed with joy and sometimes with sadness. May the Lord God grant me also a blameless Christian ending similar to the blessed repose of the godly nun Euphrosyne." This is how Fr. Anthony personally bore witness to the death of his worthy disciple—a death which testifies to her blessed life beyond the grave.*

Such were the labors of Abbot Anthony for the spiritual nourishment and salvation of his neighbors, and such were the fruits for those who unwaveringly followed his instructions.

We have seen Fr. Anthony taking care and laboring for the spiritual benefit of the Monastery's visitors, at the same time presenting himself towards them in the humble rank of an ordinary person, fleeing from all outward importance. Even more so did he take care to occupy the most humble place among the brethren in the Monastery. It was edifying and touching to watch how the venerable Elder, with the deep reverence of a child and with sincere love, regarded his older brother, Archimandrite Moses, as his spiritual father and superior. He humbled himself before Fr. Moses like the lowliest novice. Coming to him, he never entered his inner quarters without an invitation, but stood in the antechamber waiting

---

* Abbot Anthony wrote a year after her death to her sister, "K. A. is praying for all of us because her soul is alive. Some of our brethren, and also some other people, have seen your sister in dreams in a pleasant way. And I saw her in a dream as if in reality on the radiant day of Pascha. She was in church during the service, dressed unusually in a garment of inwoven gold, with her loose hair let down, and with a golden censer in her hands, censing everyone. The censer with incense signifies her prayers offered to the Lord for all. This is how your dearly beloved Katya fares at present; she is in continuous prayer to God for the salvation of our souls."

until the Archimandrite would notice him and invite him in. Entering, he did not sit down, but stood on his feeble legs until he was asked to sit down. In the presence of Archimandrite Moses and his visitors, he kept absolutely silent except when greeting someone briefly and in a low voice. When it was necessary he respectfully explained the matter involved, and every word of Fr. Moses he received without contradiction as the will of God. He did all this not under compulsion, but with sincere love in his heart. Archimandrite Moses, for his part, sincerely respected his brother and often took spiritual counsel from him, especially in the last years. He even humbled himself before Fr. Anthony in his conversation with others, saying, "He is a true monk, but I am not a monk." At the same time, as a spiritual and wise man, he did not forget the words of St. John Climacus: "The director of souls does harm both to himself and to the ascetic if he does not give him frequent opportunities to obtain crowns such as the superior considers he merits."* That is, he did not prevent Fr. Anthony from humbling himself, and treated him as a novice. Many people did not understand this, but Fr. Moses knew what Fr. Anthony's soul hungered for.

As far as the brethren were concerned, Fr. Anthony not only duly respected all of them, but as usual honored them exceedingly, showing his kindness and sincere love to everyone. His complete devotion to Archimandrite Moses, as well as the perfect oneness of soul between them, was known to all. If someone had some trouble or dissatisfaction with the Superior, that person did not hesitate to go to Fr. Anthony to seek consolation and ask for help and assistance. Fr. Anthony, in his deep humility and considering himself a stranger and outsider, never took part in any monastery affairs. He never dared to offer the Superior his advice without being asked nor did he attempt

---

* *The Ladder of Divine Ascent,* Step 4:27.

to intercede for anyone, but without deliberation he left everything to the decision of the Elder. Therefore, if one of the brethren came to him with a problem or request, Fr. Anthony simply tried to be kind to him, to console the brother, and to incline him to make peace; but he did not relay his desires to the Superior. Similarly, if someone revealed to him in confidence his secret thoughts, infirmities, or intentions, Fr. Anthony kept silent and never spoke about them to the Superior. He did not warn him, discerning this to be the devil's job, as he termed it, but left it to God's judgment. In this way, the brethren were always content with Fr. Anthony and, feeling his sincere sympathy, departed consoled and reassured. Nothing disagreeable ever resulted from their trust in him. By avoiding interference in monastery affairs and preserving good relationships with the brethren and visitors, Fr. Anthony set the best example of humility and won the hearts of all. "Behold," the Elder used to say, "many people love me very much, but I don't know why and I am quite surprised. They consider me to be a saint, whereas this saint is rotten to the core and more sinful than anyone." Another time he expressed himself this way, "I don't have anyone who wishes me evil; I love everyone and everyone loves me." Really, there was not anyone in the Monastery who did not feel consolation at the sight of Fr. Anthony, and everyone lowly or mighty paid him due respect and loved him. The Elder, Hiero-schemamonk Macarius, who reposed in 1860, had a spiritual friendship with him; it was edifying to see how they humbled themselves before each other, each showing greater respect to the other.

In 1839, Fr. Macarius, after being appointed Superior of the Skete in place of Fr. Anthony, had written to him, among other things, the following: "Father, pray for me that I will be able to accomplish at least a hundredth of what you accomplished while you were with us. I am not worthy of this position and am not familiar with these affairs." In another letter Fr. Macarius considered Fr. Anthony (and always sincerely admitted it) "to be according to seniority and wisdom older and wiser than I." In turn, Fr. Anthony sincerely acknowledged the superiority of Elder Macarius. In 1860, after the repose of Fr. Macarius, Fr. Anthony, describing his death and funeral in a letter to their common acquaintance, concluded his letter with the following words: "Here I have been living in this world for almost sixty-six years, but I have never seen such a spiritually triumphant funeral as has been celebrated for Fr. Macarius. How true is the word of God: *I will glorify them that glorify me* (I Kings 2:30). And since the Elder in this life loved everyone, so after his death he gathered together many at his grave. I don't know if we, poor in good deeds, will be deemed worthy of such a great memorial of prayer as has been granted to our blessed Elder, Fr. Macarius, whose holy soul dwells in blessedness."

In dealing with his cell-attendants and closest neighbors, Fr. Anthony distinguished himself by the same characteristics which he showed throughout his entire life. Even in giving a simple order he would say, "It seems that we need to do this or that"; and when someone once asked him why he didn't say simply, "Do this," he replied that this was his peculiar habit and that he was not able to change it.

After retiring, Fr. Anthony decided not to accept money from anyone for himself, and he very seldom broke this rule. That is, he accepted only books or offerings to buy books. He did not refuse candles and oil for icon lamps because, due to his continuous illness, often he could not go to church for Divine Services but read them in his cell, and for this purpose he lit candles before the holy icons. Sometimes when he wanted to help someone in extreme need, he asked for money for that purpose from close acquaintances. With the exception of these cases, money which he received in the mail he gave to the

Superior. If during his grave illness he agreed to accept something from people devoted to him for his absolute necessities, he often exhorted them to take back half, or at least some part, of the amount offered. Likewise, everyone who wanted to present the Elder with something necessary for his cell, he exhorted to moderate or to limit their gift; and he also divided among others what he received.

Among the younger brethren in the Monastery there was almost no one who on his nameday would not come to receive Abbot Anthony's blessing. In addition, everyone received something (and Fr. Anthony would personally send something to many): a kerchief, a booklet, or something else. To some he gave tea and sugar. It sometimes happened that the Elder, having given everything away, was left without any tea for himself. He remembered the precise date of everyone's nameday, and if he met that person, even if he were a boy or a novice, he would without fail greet and congratulate him. He was considerate to others in the minutest detail, and to all, small and great, he showed sincere love.

Fr. Anthony's life in retirement lasted twelve years, and memorable was that time for Optina Monastery because it was then adorned by three divinely-wise elders: Archimandrite Moses, Abbot Anthony, and Elder Macarius. Of these three, Abbot Anthony was to survive the others. In 1860 Fr. Macarius reposed; in 1862 Archimandrite Moses completed his course of earthly life, after which the Lord prolonged the days of Abbot Anthony, who was weighed down by many illnesses, for three more years.

6

Last Years and Death

THE REPOSE of Archimandrite Moses deeply touched the heart and affected the life of Abbot Anthony. This revealed to everyone what strong and tender love he felt for his older brother, while at the same time showing him the strictest obedience. His grief was inexpressible. During the course of the entire year, he avoided people as much as possible and devoted his solitude to the unceasing commemoration of his brother. During the first forty days he went into complete seclusion, received almost no one, and constantly read the Psalter for the newly reposed. If anyone mentioned the name of the reposed in conversation with Abbot Anthony, it brought so many tears to his eyes that the conversation had to be broken off. Several times Abbot Anthony was asked to compose notes about the life of his brother, or at least to dictate to someone what he knew about his brother, since he was the closest witness of all the ascetic labors of Archimandrite Moses and the one with whom he shared the secrets of his heart. But the Elder refused to comply with this request because, as has been mentioned, he could not remember his brother without pain of heart and tears, which gave him no opportunity to continue the conversation. Therefore Fr. Anthony never revealed to anyone the mystery of the hidden spiritual life of Fr. Moses, which was known to him alone, and he carried this mystery with him to the grave. Perhaps in so doing he fulfilled the will of the reposed—that is, after the death of Fr. Moses he did not wish to reveal what Fr. Moses had carefully hidden from everyone during his life.

Abbot Anthony did reveal to several people that his spiritual contact with his brother continued after his death. He constantly felt his presence and closeness. Their souls mystically conversed, and a day scarcely passed in which the reposed did not appear to him in a dream. Some of those dreams were especially remarkable. Fr. Moses spiritually consoled and supported his brother from the other world, and conveyed solutions to him in certain perplexing circumstances regarding Fr. Anthony as well as certain other people.

When Fr. Isaac, being at that time only a young hieromonk, was appointed, by the special arrangement and indication of God's Providence, the successor of the reposed Archimandrite Moses, the full depth of Fr. Anthony's humility of wisdom was revealed. In spite of the difference in age and the fact that the new Superior always showed much reverence to Fr. Anthony as a great spiritual man, the venerable Elder also humbled himself, as the least novice, before the new Superior. Accustomed to living not according to his own will, he went to him for the blessing to go to services and so forth and, as before, humbly waited in the Superior's anteroom until he was noticed. In general, he showed him deep reverence as to his senior; and, no matter how the Superior himself tried, he was unable to compel Fr. Anthony to change his attitude towards him. And when Fr. Isaac, out of heartfelt respect toward Fr. Anthony, made a prostration in front of him, then the Elder, too, despite his ailing legs, prostrated himself before him in reply, and thereby compelled Fr. Isaac to discontinue his prostrations. Once on one of the Twelve Great Feasts, knowing that Abbot Anthony would be coming to the refectory, the new Superior put the chair of

Fr. Anthony next to his own. Seeing this, although tired from standing on his painfully sick legs throughout the long service, the Elder humbly approached the Superior and begged that he might read the instruction from the reader's stand during the brethren's meal as he had been sometimes allowed to do by the late Archimandrite. In this way he declined the honor of sitting next to the Superior of the Monastery. Abbot Anthony now refused, even more than before, to participate in monastery affairs; and even in cases when the Superior turned to him for advice, he in every way avoided giving it, but only tried to console, reassure, and encourage him in his new cares and labor. Often, in order to strengthen and edify him, he told him how he, too, had experienced the heavy burden of the cross of being an abbot in the Maloyaroslavets Monastery.

In 1863, Abbot Anthony, in fulfillment of his long-standing desire to venerate the newly glorified Hierarch Tikhon of Zadonsk, undertook a pilgrimage to the shrine of his holy relics, and while in Voronezh also went to venerate the holy relics of St. Metrophanes. On his way he visited several monastic communities and several families devoted to him. Everywhere this splendid and holy Elder was received with ineffable joy and delight; and everyone tried to console him since he was exhausted by his old age, his illnesses, and his journey. Everywhere people showed him great reverence, which he accepted with much humility. He described his present spiritual feelings in a letter to a close friend in the following words: "By the great honor that has been shown to me *my heart is not exalted, nor are mine eyes become lofty, nor have I walked in things too great or too marvelous for me* (Ps. 130:1-2), but in the spirit of humility I beheld myself unworthy of any honor which alone belongs to the One Lord God." Blessed is he who can speak this way in sincerity of heart!

Completing this last journey not without great effort, and returning to his monastery, Fr. Anthony began more and more to retire to solitude and to prepare for his departure from this world. He said to everyone that his life was being prolonged only through the prayers of others.

Meanwhile, since the repose of the Archimandrite, the Elder had not ceased thinking of receiving the Great Schema; but, due to his deep humility, he considered it needful to test his readiness to receive it. After examining himself for two years, at the end of the third year he was ready to make the decision; and on the ninth of March, 1865, when the Elder had reached exactly seventy years of age, he carried out this decision with the blessing of the diocesan bishop. Since the Elder was sick, he was tonsured in his cell by the Superior of the Monastery, Abbot Isaac.

For a short time only, the newly tonsured Schema-abbot discontinued the reception of lay people and seldom received the monastery brethren. He devoted all of his time to ascetic labors of prayer and contemplation. Those who saw him at this time will never forget how splendid the face of the Elder looked while dwelling in quiet solitude and being delivered from conversations which had long burdened him. His face was illumined and shone with great joy, which was a result of his continuous prayer and the abundance of spiritual consolation. In general, after his tonsure into the great angelic habit everyone noticed in him much that was new. It seemed that grace abounded within him. He was constantly occupied with the thought of death. Previously he had remembered it with fear and trembling and had often been frightened with the reflection on the possibility of sudden death. And when his close ones asked him in surprise if he were really still afraid of death, he would reply that they themselves did not understand what they were surprised at, for the absence of such fear simply indicates great spiritual insensitivity. Some particular spiritual power now appeared in him, and he accepted the thought of death not only peacefully, but with great joy. In spirit he renounced everything earthly, and one could notice that the proximity of his death had been revealed to him. He previously liked to speak about death, but now he made it very clear to many people that his departure was drawing nigh.

In 1864, he plainly foretold to several people who visited him that they would not see him again, while to others he revealed that they would see him once more before his death; all of this happened exactly as he said. In November, 1864, he wrote in his own hand to one of his spiritual daughters how she should pray for her newly reposed spiritual father.*

In general, from the whole disposition of his life, from his reception of the schema down to the most insignificant details, one could clearly see that the Elder was definitely preparing for his departure. From the beginning of 1865, he stopped ordering books and refused books offered to him, saying that he no longer needed anything. He instructed one of his spiritual children to write with large letters on a poster: "Don't waste time!" and fasten it over his bed of illness as a steady reminder for others who still wanted to profit by his precepts, as well as for a reminder to himself. And indeed, he did not waste time. "Here I am at the beginning," he used to say, and began adding labor to labor, struggling like a young, healthy man.

Because of his excessive struggles, his disease and bodily sufferings grew even worse. In spite of everything, he continued to go to church as long as he could. Often the novice who served

---

* This prayer is as follows: "Look with kindness of heart, O All-hymned Theotokos, upon Thy servant who hath fallen asleep, the newly reposed (name), and pray to Thy Son and our God to remember not the sins of his youth and ignorance, and through Thy holy and all-powerful prayers vouchsafe him to reign with the saints in eternal glory. For Thou art the salvation of the Christian race and hast been given grace to pray for us."

him, seeing that the Elder, being completely exhausted, was preparing to attend the Liturgy or Vigil, tried to dissuade him from going. The Elder would humbly reply, "Forgive me for God's sake!" and would go to the temple of God leaning upon his cane, moving with great difficulty one foot after the other and groaning with pain.

On the 24th of June, the commemoration of the Nativity of the Forerunner and the feast day of the Skete, Abbot Anthony compelled himself to attend Liturgy at the skete church in order to console the brethren there. But this visit of the Elder to his beloved Skete was already his last; he was rapidly losing strength. On the 7th of July, the eve of the Feast of the Kazan Icon of the Mother of God, his final illness began with attacks of typhoid fever. This was a result of the closure of the old wounds on his legs due to scurvy, and also because of a grave dyspeptic disorder of the digestive system. It lasted exactly one month. The Abbot gave one of his spiritual daughters who visited him on the 7th of July to understand very clearly that this illness which had just begun would end with his death. When she could not restrain her tears, he looked at her expressively, smiled and said, "What can be done? Although it's a pity, still we must carry the old priest to the graveyard."

Fr. Anthony's physical sufferings were very severe. According to the word of the Lord, *He that endureth to the end shall be saved* (Mk. 13:13). It was not enough that Fr. Anthony carried on innumerable voluntary and involuntary labors during his forty-nine years of monastic life; in his last days he also had to drink the cup of excruciating physical anguish to receive greater rewards in heaven. "For it is not God's good pleasure," says St. Isaac the Syrian, "that those whom He loves should live in ease while they are in the flesh, but rather, so long as they are in this life, to abide in affliction, in oppression, in weariness, illness, contrition of heart and bodily hardships.... In these men the word of the Lord is fulfilled: *In the world ye shall have tribulation* (John 16:33), but in Me ye shall rejoice."*

Internal fever deprived the sick Elder of sleep, and he could only doze briefly from time to time. He ate almost nothing except a small amount of food or a little sip of cold water in order to quench the fever which burned within him. However, he not only endured these sufferings with singular spiritual strength, courage, and submission to the will of God, but also, amidst his fatal sufferings, he took more care for others than for himself. The illness required that the Elder remain calm, yet, not paying any attention to the exhortations of the doctors, he received all visitors as long as it was possible and was not bothered by them, constraining them himself to stay longer in order to tell them everything necessary. He even sent for devoted persons in order to explain to them his last will about something or to help them resolve some perplexity.

The Elder, conquered by love which he was unable to contain, did not care to suppress or conceal his gift of clairvoyance and his sufferings. He made haste to convey his last will and his last word to everyone for the benefit of all. As if reading everyone's thoughts, he said what was most important to each person. In a few words he embraced a person's whole life, all the most urgent needs of each soul, and gave admonitions full of such spiritual power that his words penetrated the deepest recesses of the heart and became indelibly imprinted on it. Whoever was vouchsafed to see and hear the Elder in the last days of his life will understand what we are trying to say; to the rest we are not able to describe in our limited speech the exalted, grace-filled might which charged the Elder's admonitions before his death. He tried especially to arouse spiritual vigilance and to animate in each one hope in God's mercy.

---

* *Op cit.,* Homily 36, p. 176 in Russian. Homily 60, pp. 293-4 in English.

Three days before his death, one spiritual daughter came to visit him. Seeing his grave sufferings, she was deeply afflicted both spiritually and physically, and at the same time was further worried by the thought that she might have hurt him in some way; but she did not dare to ask him any more about anything. When she entered in order to receive his blessing, the dying Elder took her by the hand and exclaimed solemnly, as if he were answering her thoughts, "Be completely assured; don't worry about anything! I am entrusting you to the protection and intercession of the Heavenly Queen; I entrust you to Her."

When the Elder was completely exhausted, he temporarily discontinued the reception of visitors or silently blessed them. In the last days he blessed everyone, giving each a small icon (more than 1,000 of them were distributed), saying, "Take it from a dying man for eternal remembrance of him."*

To some who asked him to pray for them after his death, he answered simply and affirmatively, "Very well," or "I will pray." Once, in reply to such a question from one of the skete elders who visited him, he answered, "You must pray that I obtain boldness before the Lord God." He said this so quietly and in all confidence, however, that one cannot doubt that he had already obtained what he was asking for.

Another time he answered the same person, "Isn't this some sort of temptation? Other people are afraid and fear death, but I, a sinful man, have no fear, nor am I at all afraid; on the contrary, I feel a kind of joy and peace, and I await my death like a great feast." The Elder, due to his deep humility, did not trust his own peaceful state, and as a spiritual man awaited and guarded himself against the snares of the enemy

---

* One brother, hearing that the Elder was conversing with everyone, thought: "I'll go too and have a chat." Receiving him, the Elder spoke straight to his thought, "May God bless you, but I cannot talk; I am too weak."

until the last moment of his life. Yet, by these words and his firm belief and hope in God's mercy, he unwillingly revealed what a high level of spiritual stature he had attained. "A man cannot," says St. Isaac the Syrian in his 76th homily, "acquire hope in God unless he first does His will with exactness. For hope in God and manliness of heart are born of the testimony of the conscience, and by the truthful testimony of the mind we possess confidence in God. The testimony of the mind consists in the fact that a man's conscience does not accuse him of negligence in anything within his powers that it is his duty to do. *If our heart condemn us not, then have we confidence toward God* (I John 3:21). Thus, boldness comes from the achievements of virtue and a good conscience."* These words were now fulfilled in Abbot Anthony. From his youth until deep old age he had compelled himself not only as much as was in his power, but also above and beyond his power, to work for the Lord; and now amidst his death agony, he strengthened and consoled others, as well as himself, by undoubting hope in God's mercy.

Finally, the unavoidable agony set in which usually occurs at the separation of the soul from the body, partly because the dying Elder who always liked to pray in silence was continuously talking to visitors, and partly on account of his increased physical sufferings. But even in the most difficult moments he preserved complete self-composure; one could not notice in him any trace of impatience or any similar thing.** To comply with the wish of those surrounding him he did not refuse medical help, but openly expressed that he did not hope to receive any

---

* Homily 40, p. 203 in English.

** In the beginning of his illness the Abbot saw in a dream Archimandrite Moses, who, reminding him of his own painful terminal illness, admonished him to endure his sufferings with courage until the end in order to receive great mercy from the Lord.

benefit from it. On the other hand, he accepted spiritual treatment with great joy.

On the 21st of July, seventeen days before his death, the Elder decided to receive Holy Unction while he still had some physical strength. In the last days he partook of Holy Communion daily. In addition to daily Communion, the dying Elder sought relief in unceasing prayer and also in being sprinkled with holy Theophany water, especially in his last days. He asked that not only he be sprinkled, but also his bed and all his quarters, while verses 9 through 14 of Psalm 50 be recited, beginning with the words, *Thou shalt sprinkle me with hyssop,* up to the words, *and with Thy governing spirit establish me.* When his request was strictly carried out, he was comforted and exclaimed several times, "O, how necessary this sprinkling is! How the grace of God is present!" When the Elder's sufferings increased considerably, his spiritual children who were present at the time read at his command a special prayer for the gravely ill and dying father, taken from the handwritten collection which he had personally compiled.* It became evident that

---

* Ever occupied with the thought of death, Fr. Anthony had already compiled in 1863 "A Collection of Several Prayers for our Gravely and Incurably Ill Fathers and Brothers, together with the Canon at the Departure of the Soul with the Panikhida and Prayers for the Newly Reposed." In addition to the familiar canons taken from published church books, some unpublished prayers from a handwritten collection belonging to the Florishchev Hermitage and others were also included in this collection. We present here the above-mentioned prayer, which Fr. Anthony had his spiritual children read: "Lord Jesus Christ, Son of God! Protect, save, have mercy and preserve, O God, by Thy grace the soul of Thy servant our brother (or father), monk (or priest).... Disregard the sins of his youth and ignorance, and grant him a Christian ending, blameless and peaceful; and may his soul not see the dark countenances of the evil demons, but may it be received by the bright and shining Angels, and at the time of Thy dread tribunal be merciful to him since Thou alone art God Who hast mercy and canst save

through the zealous supplications of those praying, his sufferings were alleviated each time it was read.

As long as the sick Elder still had strength, he often sang, "With the Saints give rest, O Christ, to the soul of Thy servant, where there is neither sickness, nor sorrow, nor sighing, but life everlasting." It was obvious that he awaited death from day to day. Even during his death agony, he compelled himself beyond all human comprehension to show everyone his usual friendliness and attention; and up to the last minute of his life he took care not to hurt anyone's feelings. In his soul he had already departed from everything and everyone, and his heart was not afflicted by the grief of his most devoted disciples.

Having surrendered completely to the will of God, he had, since the very beginning of his illness, no desire to prolong his life. "I desire to depart and to be with Christ, but it seems that this is not yet the will of God," he repeated several times with tears. With surprising calm, he personally gave directions for his burial. A week before his death, he ordered that his schema and the other raiment in which he wished to be buried be laid out in a place especially appointed for them. "They will be too busy then, and may dress me some other way," he remarked. Two days before his death he ordered that candles, incense, and a censer be placed on the table for the funeral service so that everything would be at hand.

When he had begun to lose his remaining strength, he remembered the brother who had made his coffin; he called someone present in the cell and started to choose what should be given to the brother as a blessing and consolation, saying, "This is for that brother who made my home [the coffin]." He distributed in advance all his belongings for a remembrance. A

---

us!" This prayer is said twelve times with twelve prostrations, or as many as one is able to do.

brother asked him for a certain thing which had already been allotted to someone else. Explaining that everything had already been decided upon, the Elder added, "There isn't anything with which I wouldn't like to part. I would like to console everyone if I could, and if it were possible I would tear myself to pieces and distribute a little bit to everyone." Talking about his absent spiritual children on another occasion, he said, stretching forth his arms, "I would like to gather them together and embrace them all at the same time."

To the diocesan bishop, the most reverend Gregory, whom the Abbot dearly loved, he left as a remembrance one of the icons from his cell. He ordered that his prayer rope be given to His Eminence Philaret, Metropolitan of Moscow. A small icon of St. Sergius, which he had received several months prior to his death from this same Elder Philaret whom he greatly revered, he wore on his chest during the entire period of his final illness.*

In his last days the Elder stopped saying anything and received almost no one. Every day he read the Canon for the Departure of the Soul. On the 6th of August, after Liturgy and the meal in the refectory, the brethren gathered in the quarters of the dying Elder and sang the troparion and kontakion in honor of the Holy Transfiguration of the Lord. Then the Superior of the Monastery read the Canon for the Departure of

---

* This icon was brought to Abbot Anthony in March, 1865, by an Optina monk who had been in Moscow. It had been wrapped personally and sealed by the Metropolitan. Receiving it, Fr. Anthony crossed himself, held it reverently, and before opening it asked, "Is this an icon of St. Sergius?" The monk who had brought it replied that he did not know. When the Abbot opened the package and unwrapped the icon, it appeared that it actually was an icon of St. Sergius clothed in schema. Since Fr. Anthony had not long been clothed in the schema himself, this surprised him. "Did you tell His Eminence that I had received the schema?" he inquired of the monk who had brought him the icon. The latter then realized that he had forgotten to mention this to the Metropolitan.

the Soul. Afterward, all present received the final blessing and received forgiveness from the departing Elder who, until his last moments, consoled everyone—some by a meek word, some by pressing their hand, some by a friendly glance—showing everyone that he recognized them.

The 7th of August arrived. It was a Saturday and the last day of the life of the long-suffering Abbot Anthony, who was ever more concentrated in expectation of his last minute. Fulfilling to the letter the Apostle's command, *Put on the whole armor of God ... that you may be able to withstand in the evil day* (Eph. 6:11, 13), many times he asked to be clothed in the full raiment of the great angelic habit. When this was not possible due to his weakness, and they were able only to place upon him the schema, then he was satisfied simply with that. Evening came, the Sunday Vigil began; suddenly the dying Elder requested to see the Superior. When he arrived, Fr. Anthony explained that he was going to die and asked for his blessing; like a true novice he did not want to start out on his final journey without the blessing of his Superior. Unquestioningly fulfilling the will of the dying Elder and in order to console him, Fr. Isaac blessed him and took leave of him forever. Then the Elder asked him to command the bell to be rung three times, but since in monasteries three strokes of the church bell ordinarily announce that someone has died, his wish seemed unusual—to announce his repose while he was still numbered among the living. Yet, in the above-mentioned collection of prayers, in the rite during the departure of the soul, it says: "Immediately they strike the church bell three times or more, announcing to the brethren that the sick brother is departing so that they might pray for him in this way." In accordance with this precept, the Elder who was still lying in full consciousness, wanted to announce to everyone in advance his approaching end. Then he asked that the

Canon for the Departure of the Soul (which is found in the handwritten collection mentioned above) be read over him. He started reading it himself, saying in his weak voice, but distinctly, "Blessed is our God, always, now and ever and unto the ages of ages. Amen."

After the reading of the canon, the dying Elder lay silently for some time. Suddenly he glanced menacingly to the left and even raised his clenched fist. One could guess that his spiritual gaze beheld a vision which was concealed from those present, yet the heart of each trembled with some incomprehensible fear.*

One of the Monastery's spiritual fathers stood close to the bed holding a cross in his hand, bending over the face of the dying Elder, waiting for his last breath. From the menacing glance and movement of the Elder, he shuddered with surprise and fear and put down his hand with the cross; but then, taking courage, he lifted the Elder's hand with the cross and made the sign of the cross three times over the departing ascetic. The Elder became calm; he quietly and peacefully sighed twice, and with

---

* See the memorable Saying of the blessed Ascetics and Holy Fathers concerning the visions before death which St. Joseph of Panephysis (Panepho) and Abba Sisoes beheld. When Abba Joseph of Panephysis was close to death and the elders were sitting around him, he, looking at the door, saw the devil sitting by the door. Calling over his disciple, the Abba said, "Give me the cane; he thinks that, being old, I won't be able to rout him." As soon as the Abba took the cane, the elders saw that the devil, like a dog, stole through the door and disappeared. It is related about Abba Sisoes that after his arrival at Clysma, he fell ill and, while sitting with his disciple in the cell, suddenly he heard someone knocking at the door. The Elder, understanding what was happening, said to his disciple Abraham, "Tell the one who knocked, 'I am Sisoes on the mountain, and I am Sisoes also when I am on my rush mat.'" The one who knocked heard it and disappeared. [Editor's note: See an identical incident in *The Life of the Righteous Youth Peter Michurin,* Platina, California: St. Herman of Alaska Press, 1980, p. 19.]

the third, barely noticeable sigh, peacefully surrendered his pure soul into the hands of God.

Extending his humility beyond the limits of this life, Abbot Anthony had said several days prior to his repose that he did not wish to be buried either in the church or even in the monastery enclosure. He designated his place of burial in the new cemetery where his spiritual daughter, the aforementioned nun Euphrosyne, was also buried and where, with the money which she donated, a sepulchre was built, and later the cemetery church. When the Elder was asked to change this location for the sake of other people, because it would be rather difficult to serve panikhidas for him there, he argued, "Am I worth panikhidas?" Not wanting to contradict him, yet finding it hard to fulfill his will, the Superior, after the repose of Abbot Anthony, asked the diocesan bishop to resolve this problem. The Bishop ordered Schema-abbot Anthony to be buried in the side-altar of the Elevation of the Holy Cross in a wing of the Kazan Cathedral, next to Archimandrite Moses—so that the brothers, who throughout their lives had labored together, would also repose together after their deaths. This was received by the Optina brethren with great joy. To fulfill the Archbishop's will, it became necessary to dismantle the burial crypt in which the remains of Archimandrite Moses rested.

The funeral was celebrated on the 10th of August, and was attended by many people who gratefully wanted to pay their last respects to Abbot Anthony. Over his grave many warm tears of heartfelt grief were shed by people who mourned the departure of the humble-minded and loving father, who during the forty-nine years of his ascetic life lived not for himself but for God and for others, and who, after his repose in the Lord, left a highly edifying remembrance. By his entire life, he proved that even in our time true monasticism is still possible and the commandments of God are not grievous. In our feeble, selfish age of little faith, great and severe ascetic deeds are possible like those about which we read in the Lives of the Saints and in the Patericons. Possible, too, is sincere and absolute (perfect) humility, sincere Christian love to everyone, and those great spiritual gifts with which the Holy Fathers of antiquity shone— for *Jesus Christ is the same yesterday and today and forever* (cf. Heb. 13:8).

PERSONAL NOTES
AND LETTERS

Vysotsky Monastery in Serpukhov

Vysotsky Monastery

St. Tikhon of Zadonsk

I

The Personal Notes of Abbot Anthony

In remembrance of events that transpired in his life, his childhood, youth; when and where he was born; who his parents and forbears were; and where and what he studied.

Bless, O Lord!

I, the unworthy one, was born in the Yaroslavl province in the city of Romanov on March 9th, 1795, on the day of the commemoration of the Forty Martyrs who suffered in Sebaste, on Friday of the fourth week of Great Lent, during the Liturgy of the Presanctified Gifts. I was born to pious Orthodox parents of the merchant class, John Grigorievich and Anna Ivanovna Putilov. At birth I was given the holy name Alexander in honor of the holy Hieromartyr Alexander, Pope of Rome, who is commemorated on March 16th. Holy baptism was conferred upon me by the priest Gregory in the holy Church of the Kazan Icon of the Mother of God. My sponsors at holy baptism were my brother Cyril Ivanovich and my sister the maiden Anysia Ivanovna.

Before birth my mother felt ill during the entire time of pregnancy; hence, at birth I was extremely ill.

But before writing about myself, I will write several paragraphs or short pages in memory of my devout parents, who, as I said, were of the merchant class from the city of Serpukhov in the Moscow province and were called Putilov by name. My forbears—that is, my grandfathers and great-grandfathers— were peasants on monastery lands belonging to the Vysotsky Monastery in the Serpukhov district. Although they were respectable people, they were extremely poor. My father was born in the village outside the Vysotsky Monastery in January, 1752, and he was named John in honor of the great ecumenical teacher and hierarch John Chrysostom, commemorated on the 27th of January. My mother was born in the same village in December of 1751 and was older than my father by a month and a half. Her parents named her Anna, in honor of the Conception by St. Anna of the Theotokos, celebrated on the 9th of December.

At ten years of age my father was left fatherless and had to care for his sister, two years his senior, his younger brother Stephen, and his widowed mother. Since there was nothing with which to pay for education, he learned to read a little in the Vysotsky Monastery under the tutelage of the blind Hierodeacon Joel. Later, at a mature age, he taught himself to write in his free time during breaks from work. Soon after his father's death, his mother took him to the linen factory of the merchant Kishein to unravel yarn at three pieces of money a week or half a piece per day. Although such pay is most insignificant, back then a half piece had some worth, equivalent to two or three kopecks today [1860's]. At that time all provisions and foodstuffs had unbelievably low prices and money was then reckoned not in roubles but in *altyns*. But nevertheless, my father felt awful because of his poverty at the time, and on one feast day he went into the grove beyond the monastery village, and there, being alone, he reflected on his bitter orphanhood, his poverty and helplessness. He cried for a long time, entreating the Lord God with tears, asking Him for help, defense, understanding and consolation. After such tearful and humble prayer, according to his account, he began to bear his orphaned lot more nobly, hoping in God's mercy. Having worked at the linen factory for such a meager wage for a year or a year and a half, he changed jobs to work in liquor sales. He worked in this field until his very death, being stationed in many places, passing gradually through every aspect of the business and receiving, according to the measure of his success, a larger and larger salary. At first he began to work for free for the training, receiving only clothing, shoes and food from his employer. Later he began to receive money, at first a fifty-kopeck coin a month, then a rouble, a rouble and a half, then three, five and ten roubles a month. When I was born in 1795 my father was then receiving a salary of 200 roubles a year, and that money sufficed for the support of the entire family which consisted of six children, my grandmother and other relatives. My father never took money on the side while working at his job, considering such income beneath him and to be thievery. For this reason, throughout his fifty years of employment, he didn't acquire any extra capital, other than the reputation of being a highly honorable and selfless man. Moreover, for his activity at his job and his selflessness, his employers began to raise his salary: after 200 roubles it was set at 300, then 500, 700, and finally 1,200 roubles a year. This was the highest salary which he was to receive in his life.

My father entered into lawful marriage at 23 years of age, that is, in 1774, with his bride, Anna Ivanovna, a native inhabitant of the same village next to the Vysotsky Monastery. The marriage was celebrated in Serpukhov, in the Church of the Holy Myrrh-bearers, in what month I don't remember. Soon after the wedding they moved to Voronezh to live. There my father was deemed worthy to speak alone in his cell with the

Hierarch Tikhon, Bishop of Voronezh, and to receive his holy archpastoral blessing.

My parents had ten children from their blessed marital union, of which four died in infancy. But five sons reached great old age, while the eldest child, a daughter Anysia, reposed in the flower of her youth at 24 years of age.

1) A son, Peter, was born in 1777 in Voronezh, whose patron saint, the Apostle Peter, is commemorated on January 16th, and in the same year he died in infancy in the city of Serpukhov.

2) A daughter Anysia was born in December of 1779 in Serpukhov; her nameday was December 30th.

3) Timothy [the future Elder Moses] was born on January 15th, 1782, in the city of Borisoglebsk [Sts. Boris and Gleb] in the Yaroslavl province; his nameday was January 22nd.

4) Cyril was born in Borisoglebsk in the Yaroslavl province on June 1, 1784. His nameday was June 9th, in honor of St. Cyril, the Wonderworker of White Lake.

5) Jonah was born in the same city of Borisoglebsk in 1786 on October 29th, and his nameday was November 5th in honor of St. Jonah, the Wonderworker of Novgorod.

6) Basil was born in the same city in 1788 on March 3, while his nameday was on March 7th, in commemoration of the Hieromartyr Basil, who ruled as bishop in Cherson.

7) Laurence was born in the same city in August of 1790; his nameday was on the 10th of the same month. He reposed in infancy during the same year and in the same city.

8) Anna was born in the same city in January of 1793. Her nameday was February 3rd, and she reposed in infancy the next year, 1794, in the same city of Borisoglebsk.

9) Alexander [the future Elder Anthony] was born on March 9th, 1795, in the city of Romanov in the Yaroslavl province.

This city stands opposite Borisoglebsk on the other side of the Volga River.

10) Peter was born in the same city of Romanov in 1797 in the month of June and his nameday was the 29th of that month, on the feast of the Chief Apostles Peter and Paul. He reposed two weeks after birth since he had been born very ill.

My father was in the true sense an Orthodox Christian, keeping all the ordinances of Christ's Holy Church. He fasted strictly during all the holy fasts as well as every Wednesday and Friday of the entire year; and annually, having made the necessary preparation for Holy Communion, he confessed and communicated of the Holy Mysteries of Christ. He remembered and honored all Sundays and feast days, going to Liturgy, in which we, his children, always emulated him unfailingly. He called his newborn children names in accordance with the practice of the Holy Church, that is, in honor of the saint commemorated on the eighth day after birth. Only two of his children, on the occasion of his absence from the city because of his job, were given names not on the eighth day, and he expressed his regret to his wife and to the priest. The father of all these children would begin to teach them grammar, reading and writing when they reached seven years of age. He didn't send any of his children to school, not because he didn't want to see us educated, but because he greatly feared that, from a teacher's oversight and from unfitting companionship, some nonsense might enter his children's young and tender hearts and might corrupt their moral character; and therefore he personally taught them. Upon leaving the house for his work he would instruct my mother, saying: "Mother, look after the children, that they learn and not simply frolic." At the time she was a real inspector of our diligence and behavior in our home school.

My father, as I have already said, was a true son of the Holy Church of Christ, and on every feast day and Sunday he would go to God's service at church and he would conduct all of us, his five sons, along with him. We would all walk together in front of him and he behind, so we walked modestly, daring neither to talk nor to look around, and in church we stood in the same manner in front of him and prayed. Father encouraged us to pay attention most of all to the reading of the Epistle and the Holy Gospel; and, so that we might listen, he would have us retell them when we arrived back home. If we could satisfactorily recount them he would be consoled, but when we would forget then he would call us inattentive. Father would stand at the *cliros* and sing during the services for he knew all the church melodies well and he had a pleasant baritone voice. Likewise, all of us, his children, would stand at the cliros and sing harmoniously. Besides this we would also sing at home not infrequently, especially on feast days. For on such days father, having rested after lunch, loved to sing spiritual *psalms*, specifically: "My spirit hastens to send up praise to the Master Most High," "O Lord, who shall abide in Thy tabernacle?" "Woe unto me who am a sinner, alas, I have no good deeds," "Behold, diligently, O man, how your time comes and death is not far off," "How lamentable is our life upon this earth," "Most beloved Jesus, sweetness of the heart," and certain other church hymns as well. We sang these extremely harmoniously in such a way that passers-by would stop outside our home and listen, for we lived in the center of the city and on the main street. But our father would not allow us to sing worldly songs in his presence.

My father had a handsome appearance; he was tall in stature, but with a slight hunch. His face was clear and noble. In his relations with all people he was respectful and affable and had a certain charm. He was intelligent and versed in the books of Sacred Scripture, Church history, the Lives of the Saints and many historical books, and he had an outstanding memory. He knew how to speak pleasantly and to the point with everyone; with spiritual people on spiritual subjects: with worldly people about worldly affairs, with merchants about business matters, with military officers about military activities, with retired soldiers about the campaigns and battles of Suvorov, with peasants about village tasks, with fathers about raising children in the fear of God, with young people about the dangers of a life of carousing, with married men about mutual agreement in family life, and so forth. These and all similar conversations were edifying and pleasant. He had the gift of supplementing conversations in an appropriate way with quotes from Sacred Scripture and with various anecdotes and modest and decent jokes, for he was of a character which, while jovial, could not tolerate any mockery. He was extremely cordial, entertaining and hospitable. Whoever happened to visit him before lunch was sure to be persuaded to remain for lunch, not to an impressive meal, but to simple home-style cooking. He would even seat simple peasants, soldiers or groundskeepers beside himself at table, and for this he was loved by all classes of people. He personally loved and respected most of all clergy and monastics, who more often than anyone visited our home.

AFTER THIS I will write down from my own memory two or three pages about the God-loving and pauper-loving humble slave of Christ, my mother, Anna Ivanovna, who was born on December 2, 1751 of pious parents, John and Catherine Golovin, of the same village outside the Vysotsky Monastery in the Serpukhov district. Until she came of age she was raised in her parents' home, learning how to run the home, cooking and sewing both linens and outer garments. She did not learn reading or writing but was devout and fervent in prayer, and from seven years of age she loved to walk almost daily to Liturgy at the Vysotsky Monastery, which was very close to her home. In the Vysotsky Monastery at that time, there lived her own grandfather, the Hierodeacon Joel, an elder of great age and holy life who was the natural father of Anna's mother. When going to Liturgy, she would often drop by his cell and bring him from her mother either a slice of fresh bread, a cooked egg, milk or a small roll. Each time her grandfather would thank her and promise rewards to her. She would ask him: "What can you reward me with?" He in reply would tell her: "I have much treasure prepared for you." She again would ask him: "Where is it? For you don't even have so much as a chest in your cell." But he would tell her that it lay under God's throne, hinting by this for her to guess that it was not material riches, which we never had in our house, but future recompense in eternal life where, for a cup of cold water, there is abundant reward. Or perhaps he foresaw, as a holy elder, her happy marital life and the bearing of children, of which three sons would enter the monastic life and become abbots and instructors unto salvation, unto the salvation of others. For the holy elders see the future more clearly than we unworthy ones understand the present. Otherwise, I do not know if I really understand this matter of my great-grandfather, the blessed Elder Joel—God knows.

My mother, having fully reached marriageable age, was given in marriage to my father, and the Sacrament of Matrimony was celebrated in the Church of the Holy Myrrh-bearing Women in the city of Serpukhov in 1774 or 1775, I don't remember which. Likewise, I don't remember who took part in arranging the marriage, but the only thing I know for certain is that God joins people together. My mother throughout her thirty-five years of married life was in the full sense a fervent and most submissive helper to her spouse, to my father. They were never heard arguing about anything between themselves, which

The town of Serpukhov:
Church of the Holy Myrrh-Bearing Women

made many people marvel at them at that time. From the beginning of her entrance into married life until the end, she occupied herself with taking care of the home. Having a hired assistant, she would busy herself with cooking, baking bread and preparing tasty varieties of *kvas* and beer, as well as with the purchase of various incidental foodstuffs. But my father loved to make the annual purchase of supplies for the house personally. Amidst all her various household tasks, my mother found the opportunity to go almost daily to the Liturgy, and at night at home she would pray fervently and for a long time to God. I often noticed this, yet did not then know how to appreciate it; but now I recall it with reverence.

Besides this, my mother, from her youth to deep old age, dearly loved Christ's poor brothers and unfortunate people, to whom she always gave as was possible, both openly and in secret. For this she always saved from the expenditures for household purchases several ten-kopeck coins and sometimes roubles (with my father's consent, of course) and would share them with the poor and lowly. One time a pauper approached her as she was returning from church, bowed down and begged, and my mother, for lack of small coins, gave a five-rouble coin or a larger one. The pauper received her offering with such appreciation that he walked behind her for a long distance with his hat off and thanked and asked God to reward her for her alms and fulfill all her good wishes. This amazed her and caused her to be ashamed to receive such great appreciation for a small mite. Moreover, Mother was humble in spirit and was not carried away by the praises offered by people. To illustrate this I will tell about one case among many. Once people began to praise her for the way she raised her children, whose politeness and modesty many liked, but Mother said in reply: "Glory be to God, I have good children, but unfortunately, they still have a long way to go to become good."

Now I will begin to write as much as I can remember about myself in the form of a diary from the first year of my birth until the most recent, or as much as I can manage, so that certain events will not be entirely erased from my memory. Although such events will not be interesting to everyone, for me they are of the utmost importance, since more than ten times in my life was I delivered from death, for which I must until my last breath thank the Lord, Who wills not the death of me, a sinner.

1795

On March 9th of this year I was born on this earth, very sickly and crying. Because of my illness I could not then drink any kind of milk, neither my mother's nor that of cows; and my mother devised to feed me rye bread, mashed into a fluid like thin pudding and sprinkled with powdered sugar. Binding it up in a thin cloth in the form of a pacifier, she gave it to me to suck. I was fed in this way for half a year. But the Lord, *Who preserveth the infants* (Ps. 114:6), preserved me alive. After half a year with this rye bread, she began to feed me with milk, from which my health began to improve.

In the same year five legal revisions regarding residency in the provinces and cities were issued throughout the Russian Empire, and I was registered in it as a half-year-old citizen of Serpukhov.

1796

At the beginning of this year I began to be able to crawl on all fours from one place to another, but I could not yet walk. Once it happened that, crawling around, I fell from a bench onto the floor and hurt myself so badly that I started to cry. Afterwards I began to be careful so that I would not fall again; therefore, I usually sat humbly on the bench, always snuggling up against the wall. A second time, in my parents' absence, our nanny, an old maid, while taking care of me dropped me from her arms onto the floor. I was quite injured and afterwards began to be very afraid of her. If she approached me, then with a child's scream I wouldn't let her pick me up. My mother, not knowing the cause of my dislike, was surprised. But after a long time the nurse told my mother about her carelessness and with tears asked her forgiveness.

1797

March 9th of this year marked two years since my birth and I began to walk, but because of the weakness of my legs and my lack of ability, I fell very often. I still did not know how to speak.

At the end of June God gave me a newborn brother Peter, who reposed within two weeks time for he was born sickly. He was my parents last child and after him there weren't any others.

This year, at the end of summer, my father with his entire family moved from Romanov to live in Poshekhonye. This city was also in the Yaroslavl Province and was located 45 miles away from Romanov.

1798

On March 9th of this year I turned three years old and I began to learn to speak, but poorly and indistinctly, like a foreigner, so that my speech was seldom understood.

In spring of this year, on May 13th, my grandmother Irina Alekseyevna reposed at 70 years of age. I can barely remember her. The only thing that has remained in my memory is how she lay in the coffin. How should I be able to remember anything, for I was then a little over three years old and that was 66 years ago [it is now 1864]? She was my father's mother, an uneducated old woman of simple upbringing, but very kind. She would take care of all of her grandchildren, would talk with us and tell us stories, which included fables and fairy tales of her own making, such as one about birds, for example. What would they do in the morning, during the day and at night? In the morning, having awakened early, they would all sing and glorify God, but afterwards they would disperse, flying on adventures in different directions. Whatever they would notice they would tell one another. For instance: "I was in a certain village and I saw one mother severely beat her unruly and disobedient son with a switch"; then another said: "When I was in such and such a city I saw one mother being very kind to her bright young son and feeding him cookies and she promised to sew him a new outfit," and all the birds would hasten to return home for the evening. Grandmother would then add to these her own admonitions, saying that we should all get up early in the morning, pray to God and be intelligent and obedient, for which we would be treated kindly with caresses; but if we were stubborn and disobedient, then mother would hit us with a switch until we cried, and so forth. All of us children so loved to listen to our grandmother's stories that when she because of poor health would not speak, then we would all ask her to tell us something. And I among these children, though I could not speak, would nevertheless beg her with bows to tell us something, crying: "A-ba, A-ba!"—that is, "Grandma, say something"—and with my childish language I would persuade her more than the other brothers to tell us a story for our consolation.

Grandmother died in the town of Poshekhonye and was buried there in the cemetery to the left side of the entrance to the holy church. May the Lord grant rest to her soul with the saints in His Heavenly Kingdom!

This summer I could already walk without the assistance of others and I sometimes received permission to walk outside on the street and play with my companions. Once they gave me a coin for some nuts and I went by myself to buy them. But in place of the nuts I saw that the proprietor had little red boots and I wanted to buy them with the coin, but the proprietor said that I would have to have more money. I ran home and collected money and in ecstasy I raced back to the merchant to buy the red boots. But he said that I still didn't have enough money. A second time I set off to collect more and I grabbed another coin, but the merchant demanded yet more money. I became so incensed at him because of his demand for more money that I called him a cheat and ran away. So as to pacify me, he gave me the boots without any money, but I stubbornly refused to take them. It was an incident that showed in me, for the first time, irritability and stubbornness.

During that same summer one further remarkable incident happened to me: one time while walking on the street, I saw outside a tavern a coachman playing a balalaika, another dancing and a third singing songs. This music pleased me so strongly, that, asking the coachman for the balalaika, I ran home with it and began to play on it, jumping around and crying out. My mother was so astonished and grief-stricken by this that she punished me: "O you wretched buffoon! I will teach you to cry, not to dance," and right away she hit me with a switch. But when she began to break the balalaika and throw it into the stove, I was so distressed by this, sobbing and weeping inconsolably, that from grief I fell to the ground and fell fast asleep. This first temptation of the adversary revealed to me that from youth or childhood the heart of man yearns more for what is base than for what is good.

In the autumn of that year an unforgettable guest—smallpox—visited me, not through vaccination, but naturally from a cold, and it nearly deprived me of my life. When it began to develop and mature, it produced hard and intolerable pustules and I began to pick at the pox with my hand. But my mother, afraid that I might disfigure myself, bound my hands with a kerchief. Then I cried and complained: "What did I do to you? Why are you tying me up?"

But at the end of that year, just after Nativity, my parents went on pilgrimage to the Monastery of St. Adrian, which is three miles distant from Poshekhonye, to thank St. Adrian for my recovery. There after Liturgy and a moleben, the Superior, Abbot Moses, invited my parents and me to his cell and offered us tea and milk, a gesture which has remained in my memory to this day and for which may the Lord save him!

1799

On the first day of February early in the morning, my parents, by order of my father's employer for the same business of collecting liquor revenues, set out from Poshekhonye for Romanov. The whole family arrived in Romanov on February 2nd, and stayed at their former apartment in the home of the elderly woman Alexandra Ivanovna Babushkina.

On March 9th of that year I turned four. At the time, I had an unusually refined sense of hearing, so that every night I would wake up with the first peal of the bells for Matins and would wake up my parents and my brothers, saying: "Ding! Dong! Angels are singing, get up to pray!" This went on for several months. But when I began to see that certain of my brothers started to get angry at me for this and would not get up, then I too, seeing their example, started to grow careless, and like them, would sink back to sleep and would sleep the whole night through without waking up. But from the first day of the Holy Pascha of Christ, I started to always walk to Liturgy whenever there would be a service, without anyone accompanying me. I always stood in the holy altar where the priest treated me warmly. He would seat me on a cushion so that I would not get tired and would sometimes give me antidoron [a piece of bread blessed at the Liturgy] and at other times a whole prosphoron [loaf used at the Liturgy], in this way training me to always come to the service. And if I would notice that anyone was approaching to receive Communion of the Holy Mysteries, then I would also approach and he would give me Communion. Once it happened that when I approached the priest and began to ask for a prosphoron for myself, the priest asked me: "What's this, brother, haven't you eaten breakfast?" And I was so offended at this question of his that I left the church for home and, having arrived home, I complained to my father about the priest: "Papa, I started to ask the priest for a prosphoron, but he said to me, 'What, brother, have you not eaten?' Why did he have to ask about this? When he is asked, he is supposed to give and not question." I had only just finished my complaint when the priest came to our house with a prosphoron to make peace with me. This incident marks the first time that I had acted capriciously, and may the Lord preserve me from ever doing it again!

In the course of this year there were two incidents that occurred in which I nearly lost my life. Once my mother went to the river for something, for our apartment was on the very shore of the river. I ran after her, along the shore near the river, and I began to gather and place in the lap of my shirt various pebbles and shells. Then, bending farther over, I tried to get a little stone from the water and I fell headfirst into the water. But the Lord, *Who preserveth the infants* (Ps. 114:6) saved me from drowning. For my mother grabbed me at once by the shirt, pulled me out and carried me home crying in her arms. When I dried off she then gave me a switching so that I might not dare to run after her again without asking permission.

The second incident was as follows: I walked out beyond the gates of our yard onto the street with some young boys my age and several older than me. They led me to an abandoned lot in which nettles, burdock and henbane were growing and, taking the seeds out of the henbane, they forced me to eat them, saying: "Eat, brother, this is poppy seed." And from this poisonous plant my face and entire body turned as red as a bandanna. I felt an inner fever, dreariness and delirium, and kept repeating the very words which I had said while walking with the boys and eating the henbane. This continued for several days. But I was given scalded milk to drink, and, by God's mercy, I remained alive. After this incident I was afraid to go beyond the gates lest something similar happen to me. If I was sent out for a walk, I refused, saying like a wise boy: "There are insolent boys out there shouting and fighting, and if you associate with morons you yourself will become a moron." Therefore, without going outside the gates, I found satisfaction for myself in walking about the courtyard and in the garden. Once, in the garden, having pulled a carrot from the bed, I began to eat it and it seemed to me as sweet as sugar. Then I thought: when I become rich, I will always eat carrots. I told my mother about this innocent wish of mine and she, smiling, promised to plant a whole garden of carrots every year, and I took great delight in my future bliss of always being able to eat carrots.

At the end of this year, during the holy days between Nativity and Theophany, the marriage arrangements began in our home for the marriage of my sister Anysia Ivanovna.

1800

At the beginning of this year my sister Anysia Ivanovna, against her wishes, by the will of my father, was betrothed in marriage to a merchant's son from Poshekhonye, Cosmas Dementievich Krundishev. Her desire, however, was to enter a convent, to join her cousin, the Nun Maximilla Ivanovna. But my father would not consent, and the marriage was celebrated on January 30th on the feast of the Three Hierarchs in the Church of the Kazan Icon of the Mother of God in the city of

Romanov. My sister was twenty years old at the time. I stood in church, watched the wedding, and wept. After the crowning, the priest, in his robes and with cross in hand, led the bride and groom accompanied by singing to their house, which was located not far from the church. After coming to the house, the priest removed the crowns from the newlyweds, took off his vestments and blessed the banquet table. Then began the serving of treats, followed by the feast. The bride and groom were seated at the foremost place and all the guests sat on the sides. With each course a different wine was served; there was a shot of liquor for every guest, as was the custom at that time. I was seated next to the buffet on a bureau. Without batting an eye, I would look at the bride and each time would take from the tray a glass of sweet wine that had not been entirely finished. Then, bowing to the bride from afar, I would drink to her health. I drank so much that I collapsed on the bureau and passed out. I did not hear how I was carried off to bed. This was the first time I had gotten drunk in my life. After the wedding all the guests departed for home. On the third day the newlyweds headed to their city, Poshekhonye, while we in our home, left without my sister, felt a certain kind of emptiness.

On the 9th of March of this year I celebrated my fifth birthday. At that time I would always walk to church whenever the Liturgy was being celebrated and would always stand in the holy altar. One time my father, stroking me gently, asked: "What am I to prepare you for?" that is, for what kind of profession. "For the merchant trade, for some kind of craft, or for civil service?" I replied: "Papa, I want to be a priest." My father replied to this: "They will not make you a priest if you don't study; and around me you're a little dimwit, you don't know anything." But I objected: "Papa, the priests don't do anything in the altar, they just sit; only the readers and deacons read and sing." In this conversation I first expressed the desire to enter the religious calling. Afterwards, when I played at home with kids my age, they would dress me as a priest. In place of an *epitrachelion* [priest's stole] they would put a towel over my neck, and on my shoulders a large unfurled scarf in place of a *phelonion* [large ceremonial vestment of a priest]; in place of a censer I took a small ball, tied a shoelace to it, and censed everyone. And when they gave me a cookie or an apple, I would cut it into small pieces and, placing it on a plate, distribute it in place of antidoron and bless with my hand.

Once in the summer on a Sunday I fell into a sinful temptation which made me ashamed. I came to church very early before the service. The sexton rang the bell for the Liturgy while the priest was reading prayers. Then the priest began to put on his vestments, but there weren't any prosphora in the altar yet. For this reason the priest gave me a small bag and sent me to his wife for prosphora, since their house was very close to the church. The priest's wife placed the prosphora, which had just been taken out of the oven, into the little bag and gave them to me to carry to church, and I, while walking along the road, ate one of the warm prosphora and carried the rest to church, giving them to the priest. He, in turn, placing the prosphora on a plate, saw that one prosphoron was missing and asked me: "Could you, brother, have eaten a prosphoron along the road?" I was too ashamed to acknowledge my sin and I lied, saying: "Batiushka, I really didn't eat one." This was my first lie.

In the middle of the month of August my father and my two oldest brothers, Timothy and Cyril, for reasons unknown to me were fired from work by their boss. For this reason my father, buying a horse and wagon with harness, went to Moscow to find himself a job, taking with him my three brothers Timothy, Cyril and Jonah. More than a month passed and there hadn't been any news from them. Therefore my mother, being extremely worried about them, doubted if they were even alive or thought that perhaps some misfortune had befallen them along the road. On October 1st, the feast day of our church dedicated to the Protection of the Mother of God, her doubts about their being alive were confirmed by an unexpected superstitious occurrence. Early that morning a hen had run into the kitchen and, flying up on the table in front of an icon, had crowed like a rooster. Because of this incident, my mother, being severely frightened, surmised that my father was no longer among the living, and for this the poor hen's head was cut off. But the next day my mother received a pleasant letter stating that my father was alive and had obtained an employer in commercial trade for my two older brothers, Timothy and Jonah, and hoped to find a job for himself as well. Because of this, my mother was very grieved that she had cut the poor hen's head off. What could be done? The proverb puts it well: Live and learn—and don't believe superstitious nonsense. In November my father informed us that he had been hired together with my brother, Cyril Ivanovich, for the post of liquor revenue collector in the city of Uglich in the Yaroslavl province, to which our entire family moved from Romanov. We arrived on November 27th, on the feast of the Icon of the Mother of God "Of the Sign," and stayed in an apartment belonging to the reader of the Church of the Resurrection, John Yakovlevich. The Church of Christ's Resurrection had formerly belonged to the monastery by the same name, which had been liquidated in 1764, and the church had been converted into a parish church. Above the holy gates of this monastery there was a chapel in which a wonder-working Icon of the Mother of God "Of the Sign" had been located, and the chapel stands to this day for the sake of the wonder-working Icon.

The Resurrection Monastery in Uglich as it looks today.

Aᴄᴛᴇʀ ᴛʜɪꜱ I shall write a few lines in remembrance of the towns of Romanov and Borisoglebsk. Romanov is located right on the Volga River, on the left bank of the river, while Borisoglebsk is located opposite Romanov, on the right bank. In both towns all the inhabitants are schismatics [Old-Believers or Old-Ritualists] and they never go to the churches, so there is no one to place candles in front of the holy icons. Therefore the clergy endure great want in finding food for themselves. On feast days at the Divine services in the churches, the only ones present would be those people who had been assigned to reside there, in addition to soldiers and sundry passers-by.

Among the inhabitants, only the poor were worthy of note, for, walking through the town, they would beg alms beneath the landowners' windows with prayer, saying: "O Lord Jesus Christ our God, have mercy on us! Father (the name and patronymic of the owner) and Mother (the name and patronymic of the mistress of the house) with your kind children, give holy alms to me, a lowly orphan (or a lowly widow, or a sick old man, or a cripple)." When they would be given alms, they would say: "May God grant you good health, and your parents the Heavenly Kingdom." When chained prisoners would walk by two's and three's to gather alms, they would recite the same words as the beggars and would sing melodiously. If an indigent person would beg alms without prayer, he wouldn't be given anything and the people would say: "You obviously aren't a Christian. You don't know God!" I liked this custom of the Romanov beggars then, and I have written it down in this little book so as to remember it.

1801

During the first days of January of this year my parents received news from Poshekhonye that God had given my sister,

Anysia Ivanovna, a newborn daughter, Tatiana Cosminich, which made my parents happy.

On the 9th of March I turned six.

On the night of the 12th of March, the Sovereign Emperor Paul Petrovich reposed in St. Petersburg. On the 18th of the same month, in the cathedral church in the city of Uglich, the Imperial decree was read to the entire city concerning the Sovereign's repose and the ascension to the throne of the Sovereign Emperor Alexander [I] Pavlovich. All the clergy, military and civilian officials, and other citizens were led in taking the oath of allegiance. They all signed the oath list in their own handwriting, including my father and my brother Cyril.

This year Holy Pascha fell very early, on the 24th of March; there was a lot of snow and it was very cold. Therefore, parishes had not yet moved from the heated, winter churches to the cool, summer churches. A new caftan, light-blue in color, was sewn for me for this feast. Although I still had not learned to read, I would stand at the cliros and sing with the softest child's voice: "Lord, have mercy!" I liked most of all to help out the reader, to hand him something or get something for him. Then on the Sunday of the Myrrh-bearing Women, they began to move from the winter church to the cool, summer church and I helped carry books, candles and incense. I was given an icon lamp full of oil to carry and, out of haste, I tripped and fell on the floor. The oil spilled all over me and ran all over my new blue caftan. In grief I went home, where my father bawled me out for my carelessness and said, "What a stupid candle-lighter you are! You broke the lamp and spilled the oil on yourself. Now you can go around in a spotted caftan." But my mother consoled me, saying that she would wash out the soiled places and sew it again, which she soon did.

In the city of Uglich there were fifteen churches in all. On the parish patronal feasts I would go to the vigils and to the Holy

The city of Uglich: the palace where St. Demetrius
the youth-prince was murdered.

Liturgy, for I dearly loved the solemn feast day services, the singing, the illumination of the church with many candles, the brocade vestments on the clergy. I took great delight at the violet velvet *kamilavka* on the cathedral archpriest, for at that time he was the only clergyman in the city who had this distinction. Therefore, in every procession which went from the Cathedral to the parish churches on their feasts, and also in every procession around the city, I was always present, never feeling tired.

In the city of Uglich, near the Cathedral, there is an ancient stone palace in which the holy right-believing Crown Prince Demetrius, who was slain at the order of [Boris] Godunov, lived from his earliest years with his mother. I had been in this palace many times, but his holy relics had been translated from Uglich to Moscow and displayed in the Kremlin in the Cathedral of the Archangel Michael. Later I was able to go there many times to venerate them.

In the course of that year, calling upon God for help, I began to learn to read and write. My brother Basil was appointed to be my teacher and I began to study the alphabet under his direction.

1802

This year I continued to study; I learned the *Horologion* and, becoming familiar with it, I finally began to learn the Psalter.

At the beginning of the month of October, my father travelled to Moscow to purchase wine, taking my brother Basil with him and leaving him there with my brother Timothy in order to find employment.

1803

On January 30th, my father, by the order of his employers, left the city of Uglich and moved with his family to the provincial seat of Yaroslavl, where he safely arrived on February 1st.

In May, God granted my sister Anysia a new daughter, Maria, who died within several weeks.

On November 1st, my sister Anysia fell ill with the flu, and on this account she offered repentance to the Lord God and communicated of the Holy Mysteries of Christ. Then she begged forgiveness of everyone who was there and also, by letter, of all of us. In full consciousness and with hope in the merits of our Redeemer, the Lord Jesus Christ, she reposed to the singing of funeral hymns between the 8th and 9th of that month at 11:00 o'clock at night. May her memory be eternal! She was a kind and peace-loving person in every respect. I travelled to her burial with my parents from Yaroslavl to Poshekhonye. She was buried in that town on the 12th day of that month.

My sister Anysia Ivanovna lived three years, nine months and nine days in wedlock and her life lasted 23 years, 10 and a half months. She left behind her only daughter, three years of age, who was given over to the care of my mother.

1804

At the beginning of this year, calling upon God for help, I began to learn to write under the direction of my brother Cyril, which I continued to do the entire year.

At the end of November, my brother-in-law, the husband of my sister Anysia, Cosmas Dementievich, left St. Petersburg for the Sarov Monastery to dedicate himself to the monastic life.

On December 31st, my father, through the mediation of my brother Timothy, was given his release from the Serpukhov civilian commission with all his family, and assigned to the Moscow commission in the third guild of merchants.

1805

On the 5th of May, my father received from Moscow a letter from my brothers Timothy and Jonah, in which they wrote that they had left their employers due to the impossibility of working under them under any circumstances, because of their extreme strictness and their unfairness. They wrote that they had in mind another employer, an extremely kind man of pious morals, to whom they had given their word that they would work for him. But before this they planned to journey to Kiev to venerate the relics of the holy God-pleasers, and from there to come and spend some time with us. But things turned out otherwise. In Moscow they told their relatives that they were going to visit us. For some reason they had taken passports for three years without the knowledge of my father and, instead of Kiev, they wound up someplace else. They had long had the desire to abandon all the cares of this world, to dedicate themselves to the Lord God and to live a secluded monastic life, but they had kept delaying for a long time. At last, finding the right opportunity, they put their plan into action. For this reason, they left Moscow for Sarov Monastery in the Temnikov region of the Tambov province. Upon their arrival there on the 13th of May, they were received by Hieromonk Isaiah, the Superior, who then assigned them an obedience. We hadn't heard any news from them for half a year so we doubted that they were alive. Finally my father received a letter from them in November, in which they asked forgiveness for causing him grief, asking at the same time a blessing from him on their path of salvation. Reading this letter, my father became extremely grieved with them. Not only did he not bless them to become monks, but he even forbade them to tarry there long, insisting rather that they return to him as soon as possible. But the merciful God made totally different provisions for them, as we will later see.

At the end of that year, I finished my study of reading and writing without having attended any school. For the entire course of my studies, which had lasted four and a half years, I had studied in my parent's home with the help of my aforementioned brothers. In science I was quite dull, as well as extremely lazy, on account of which I had to study for a long time.

1806

His Eminence Paul, Archbishop of Yaroslavl and Rostov reposed on March 19th. His funeral procession was extremely stately and worthy of interest. It took place on the 28th of that month. He was buried in the Yaroslavl Dormition Cathedral alongside the right choir.

On April 17 my father and his family were given a certificate of appreciation from all the representatives of the Moscow Municipal Commission, signed by the chief members and with the Commission seal affixed to it.

On September 1st my father's employers gave his accounts to another agent, because of which my father agreed to go to work for the provincial Governor-General Kolychev. On the 28th of October, he set out from Yaroslavl for his assignment in the city of Mologa in the same province, arriving there on the 30th of the same month; then he called us to come as well. I left Yaroslavl with my mother on the 18th of November with all our belongings, and we arrived on the 20th of that month, completing our journey safely.

We lived in Yaroslavl three years, nine months and seventeen days. During that entire time, I studied reading and writing. I also performed the duties of lamplighter in the Church of the All-Merciful Savior in the city, where I read the hours and sang quite well. I rang the bells for the services and assisted in the altar in such a way that I was cherished by the

Saint Demetrius, Prince of Uglich

Priest James, who became my spiritual father, and I received as a reward from him two prosphora every day.

1807

On September 10th, my father was sent from Mologa on a mission to Moscow to purchase various supplies for liquor accounts, for his own needs. He rode on company horses, taking me along with him for the experience. Having travelled thirty miles the first day, we spent the night in a settlement by the river Yukhta, at a place where there had recently been a fire. In the morning, we thought to leave very early. Having paid the landlord for the room, my father walked out of the cottage. Somehow his right foot stumbled on the stairway; he gouged some of the skin off his shin, and it was injured so painfully that he thought that he had broken it. Upon examination, however, it appeared whole. Rather than turning back, we travelled onward out of ignorance. We shall see that this caused an ailment in my father's leg, a most severe ailment of which he would later become a victim and from which only death itself would deliver him.

Early on the morning of the 15th of that month we arrived at the Holy Trinity-St. Sergius Lavra, where we stood through four Liturgies in a row. On account of the solemn festival then taking place, I was deemed worthy to see a great man revered and respected by all: the blessed archpastor Platon, Metropolitan of Moscow.

After the moleben I walked around the monastery, looking at everything with delight, but especially at the exquisite bell tower built in Gothic style, which was of great height with columns and various arches. At every step something new and highly curious presented itself to my gaze. After the meal, around Vespers, we resumed our journey, and finally, on the 16th toward evening, we arrived in the capital city, Moscow, where we stayed until the 26th of that month. During that time, we stayed at our relatives, visited people, saw noteworthy places and visited churches. At each step I encountered something pleasant or sorrowful which made an impression on my mind. Wherever I would turn my gaze, I encountered novelty in the various sights which I beheld. All of it caused the young and inexperienced provincial boy to wonder and experience great delight. Finally leaving Moscow, we arrived safely in Mologa on October 2nd in the morning.

On December 14th, my brother Basil arrived from Moscow, and he was hired to monitor liquor sales.

On the 23rd of the same month, my brother Timothy came from Sarov Monastery to my father to ask forgiveness for the action which had grieved my father, as well as to ask his blessing and his release from the provincial authorities, freeing him of civil obligations in order live in a monastery.

1808

My father, after his return from Moscow, was extremely distressed about his leg. He could hardly even walk about the room. From the time of his return a month had gone by, and he had not managed to get a doctor to come, and he needed advice and help. All he heard was the stupid advice of some old women, and he followed their advice without observing any guidelines or keeping to any diets; and whatever someone might say, he did it. As a result, gangrene developed in the wound of his ailing leg. Seeing this, we urged him to summon a doctor, who then began to help him. Thanks be to God! Within a month the gangrene left his leg. If we had delayed even a little bit more, he would have suffered painfully from it. But then another misfortune struck. His sound leg became more infected than the other; it began to swell and turn red, and he became very weak. He began to listen to other people's advice and took various drugs which made the infection worse rather than better. Then he no longer had recourse to the doctor and placed all his hope on God's will.

At this same time my brother Timothy demanded that my father release him to enter the monastic life. My father, after long opposition and debates quoting from the texts of Holy Scripture, being unable to cause Timothy's desire to waver, in the end freed him, blessing his intention. He gave power of attorney to his uncle, I. I. Golovin, to testify for him at the Mologa municipal court and to relay to the Moscow civil commission a request to provide certification of release, bearing witness that he had been freed because of the weakness of his health. He did not want to release my brother Jonah under any circumstances, saying: "He is young, and he has been talked into it. I myself want to see him, to speak with him, and to block his intention with parental severity."

My brother Timothy, receiving his release and blessing from my father, left Mologa for Moscow on the 13th of January to request his release from the Moscow Civilian Commission.

On May 30th, my brothers Timothy and Jonah came to us from Sarov to request, for Jonah, a release from my father and his blessing for the monastic life.

In the month of June, my father had begun to suffer so much from the pain in his leg that he had already begun to despair of his life. During the day, when the pain would leave him somewhat, he would be bothered to an extreme by flies. At night the affliction would torment him to death; he would ache in all his members and have shortness of breath and could only breathe through his left nostril. Seeing such a change within himself, he began to prepare for death. This was sufficient for him to remember the words of the Holy Scripture which the Holy Apostle James teaches in chapter five of his Epistle to believers in the Lord Jesus:

Is any sick among you? Let him call for the elders of the church; and let them pray over him, anointing him with oil in the name of the Lord: And the prayer of faith shall save the sick, and the Lord shall raise him up, and if he have committed sins, they shall be forgiven him (James 5:14-15).

He called for a priest. He brought forth repentance to the Lord God and was communicated by the priest of the Most Pure and Life-creating Divine Mysteries of Christ. Then Unction was served over him, anointing him with oil in the name of the Lord.

On the 18th of the month, very early in the morning, our father gathered us his children together in order to bless us all individually. The beginning of his fatherly blessing upon us was as follows: *Come, ye children, hearken unto me, I will teach you the fear of the Lord* (Ps. 33:11). Then he started to instruct us, discussing which responsibilities we must have regarding God, society, parents and ourselves. He commanded us to flee the passions and fear to do evil, to love one another, to bear difficulties and above all to be virtuous. "If you act thus," he said, "you will fulfill the law of Christ and preserve the tradition of your father. Through a base life of vice, you will bring upon yourselves in this life the wrath of God, being unsuccessful in everything, and in the future life you will have eternal torment, remorse and the defiling of the conscience. Thus, my beloved, you can see your father's example and conclude how I have sullied myself in my life. For this, the Merciful and Righteous God has chastised me with illness; he has taken from me the free movement of my body, my pronunciation of words and my breathing. Beware, lest ye be tempted, and through falling into temptation be punished and deprived of all the eternal good things prepared for those who love Him."

Then he began to bless each of us, one at a time, laying his hands upon our heads. He blessed all of us with icons of the saints. He ordained that my brother Cyril Ivanovich be as our father and provider, entrusting my brother Basil and myself to his care and commanding us to be obedient to him in everything, to revere and love him as we did my father himself. He likewise entrusted to him my brother Jonah, saying: "You can do as you like, you may release him to enter a monastery or you can retain him; it is no longer my affair." My brother Cyril thus spoke: "Since he has placed in his heart a firm intention to dedicate himself to the secluded monastic life, then I, on my part, will not divert him from this intention." My father, seeing this, blessed his intention, only asking him to remain as his guest a little longer.

Behold how our merciful God, by His Providence, arranges the salvation of our souls! Formerly, my father did not even want to hear that my brothers wanted to be released to live the monastic life, but in his illness he blessed them.

On July 20th, from extreme inattentiveness, I received a wound from which I suffer to the present day.

In the same month my father began to improve little by little from his illness. He gave my brother Jonah his formal release, recorded in the Mologa municipal court on July 22nd; and finally, blessing them both, he let them go to Moscow to obtain release from all societal obligation for entrance into the monastery. My brothers left Mologa for Moscow on August 8th in the evening.

During the month of October, I was extremely sick. My left shoulder began to swell and turn red, causing me sharp pangs and other pain; for three weeks I had no sleep. I applied various medications at the advice of others. Women, especially, tried fervently to relieve me of the pain, but to my great misfortune, it kept increasing. I found myself forced to obtain help from a doctor, who began to help me with his skill. At first, they applied an herbal plaster on my shoulder in order to open up the sore. I kept it in place for more than a week, but there wasn't any benefit to be seen, and it increased the pain and swelling. The doctor, seeing that there was little success in opening the infection, applied an arsenic plaster so as to cause the infection to open more quickly. I applied this mixture to my shoulder for three days and I was barely able to endure having it on. But thanks be to God Who sent down to me help and healing! The wound on my shoulder opened. So much material came out of it that even now it is impossible to imagine. The skin pulled away from the bone and I thought that perhaps the bone had rotted through. *With chastisement hath the Lord chastened me, but He hath not given me over unto death. What shall I render unto the Lord for all that He hath rendered unto me?* (Ps.117:18, 115:2).

During my illness I conceived the desire to devote myself to the monastic life, and I disclosed it in a letter to my older brother, Timothy, urging him to counsel me about my desire. But, to my misfortune, the preliminary draft of my letter fell into the hands of my brothers Cyril and Basil, who, wanting me to be punished for such a desire and for other parts of my letter about them, placed my letter in front of my father at a convenient moment, so that he could read it. Having read it, he became extremely displeased with me, and, as my father, wanted to punish me for such a deed. I, as his son, immediately reconciled myself with him and again, as before, got along with both my father and my brothers.

1809

At the beginning of January, my father was almost completely delivered from his ailment. He began to walk about freely, to eat food and speak as if he were healthy, which caused us to rejoice and to thank God.

On the 19th, after dinner, at about 11:00 o'clock in the evening, my father felt a fever and pain in his head. He began to pray the evening prayers to God. Suddenly, a lot of phlegm came up, on account of which he choked and began to cough. He was tormented the whole night with fever and choking and barely made it through the night. My father remained in such a state until the 25th, becoming weaker and more feeble from hour to hour. In such a short time his face and voice changed so much that one could hear what he said only with difficulty. He was in the most perilous condition he had ever been in. Seeing this, we advised him to be cleansed of his sins through repentance and Communion of the Body and Blood of Christ the Saviour. Our father accepted this advice from us with pleasure and carried it out fully in the morning of the 25th after Matins. In the evening on that day I entreated God to grant him alleviation of his afflictions. At the very same time my mother came up to him and said, "Where do you bless Alexander [to go]?" He, summoning his faltering powers, said: "To God." She repeated to him: "In what occupation do you command him to live? With his brothers, or in some other?" He at last uttered: "That he would fear God." I was extremely pleased by this, that my father had entrusted me to God and to no one else, had ordered me to give myself to His most Holy Providence, had ordered me to seek in Him a Helper amidst sorrow and in all my needs, for *none of them shall do wrong that hope in Him* (Ps. 33:22). I understand his last words to me in this sense: that wherever he might live, let him always fear God. This was his last testament to me, the unworthy one and worst of all his sons.

On the 26th at 10:15 in the morning, fully conscious but in great weakness and pain in all his members, my father reposed into the eternal and never-ending life, at 57 years of age. Grant, O God, eternal rest to him who has fallen asleep. I am consoled only by the fact that my father died as a good and true Christian should, offering repentance to the Lord God for the sins he had committed in his life, and was vouchsafed to partake of the Most

Pure and Life-creating Mysteries of our Lord, God and Saviour Jesus Christ. He reposed during the Liturgy itself, when the deacon exclaimed: "Let us stand aright, let us stand in fear, let us attend that we may offer the holy oblation in peace." [From the Anaphora of the Divine Liturgy.] At this same moment my father stood before the Judge of the living and the dead, the Lord Jesus Christ. One can actually reflect thus, as I with my stupid and inadequate reason now understand: "For the sake of Mine *elect will I shorten the time* that they might receive salvation; *blessed are they that die in the Lord* (cf. Mark 13:20, Rev. 14:13). And my father is blessed for he was granted to receive a good, blameless ending of his life. Woe to him whose soul is wrested by the demons at his departure from this world, for to him the Divine voice will resound: "In that which I find you, in that will I judge you."

On the very day of his repose, about four hours before he departed, he shouted in the morning: "Alexsasha!" I appeared before him and inquired what I could do for him. He said, "Put my shoes on me and dress me." I did everything as he instructed; I put his shoes on, dressed him in a jacket and combed his hair. Then he requested tea, of which he drank a small cupful. He asked: "What day of the week is it, Wednesday or some other day?" I answered that it was now Tuesday. But he didn't say anything else to me after this. From this one can see that although his end was near, he nevertheless remembered that his patron saint was to be commemorated on Wednesday the 27th [of January]. But what could be done? It was pleasing to God to deprive him of life before his nameday.... On the 28th, according to our Christian duty, my father was carried after the early Liturgy to the cemetery, to the Church of All Saints, after which the rite of burial was celebrated by several priests together and he was buried at that church near the altar, at the foot of the mausoleum of the merchant Kazanin....

Church of the Korsun Mother of God, Uglich (built in 1730).

2

The Letters of Alexander Putilov
(THE FUTURE ABBOT ANTHONY)
to His Brother Timothy
(THE FUTURE ELDER MOSES)

⌁ LETTER ONE ⌁

CHRIST IS RISEN!
Most kind brother, Timothy Ivanovich!

May you be saved in the Lord! I have the honor of congratulating you with the approaching feast of Pentecost. May the Lord God grant you to spend it with perfect salvation of soul, which I wish for you with my whole heart.

I thank you for your letter, which I was fortunate to receive in good condition. But I only ask your forgiveness that I was not able to notify you earlier about receiving your letters—at one point there was no time, at another I was overcome by laziness, and at another I was near death. And now I'm barely alive; my face is all swollen, I feel great pain in my head and I don't know with what to treat it. On the feast day of the Bright Resurrection I could barely make the trip to see my father. I can personally state together with the Prophet: *Many are the scourges of the sinner, but mercy shall encircle him that hopeth in the Lord*

(Ps. 31:10). Such are the circumstances I am enduring in the city of Mologa. Often a hundred-year-old man has not seen as many illnesses as I, a fifteen-year-old, have. But it's true and one can say: for every kind of sin, there is a corresponding punishment—the greater the sins, the greater the punishment. This is all applicable to me.

Beyond this there is nothing more to write, than to wish you salvation of soul and health of body. I remain your most humble servant, ever praying for you, sinful Alexander Ivanovich Putilov. I bow to the ground before you.

April 12th, 1809. Mologa.

✢ LETTER TWO ✢

My Most Kind Batiushka, Father Timothy!

Bless! The new year has come. As is our custom at the arrival of the new year, as one friend to another I send you my best wishes for it, as I would with any new thing. And I, following this custom rooted in us from time immemorial, am sending you this epistle that I have written. And moreover, from my sincere and fraternally loving heart, I wish for you, my most beloved one, that the Right Hand of the all-good and righteous God, blessing you in this new year, would pour out upon you streams of His new blessings, serving for the salvation of your soul, and for the strengthening of your bodily powers: for your eyes, that they would not see vanity; for your lips, that they would not speak lies; for your hands, that they not only bless those who bless you, but also those who do evil and nasty things to you; for your feet, that they would walk in the ways of the commandments of the Lord and fearlessly tread upon the serpent, the scorpion, and on all the powers of the malevolent enemies and trample down all their snares. All of this I wish from the depths of my sensitive, sincere, brotherly heart, which is filled with love. Please cover any shortcomings with your loving condescension. For it is written: *It is hard indeed to devise songs harmoniously put together* (Irmos, Ninth Ode of the Second Canon of the Nativity).

I have become so guilty before you that I am ashamed even to justify myself, not having a worthwhile excuse. I beg your love—consign my deed to oblivion and remember it no more, and forgive me, your very sinful brother. Well, kind Batiushka, unfortunate circumstances have forced me to be here, and to live here up to this day. God knows why I live here, for whom I am waiting and what to expect, yet I myself don't know. God, due to the iniquities that have multiplied in the towns and villages, has sent His wrath upon the people, that they might humble themselves before Him and believe undoubtingly in Him. For He is good and meek towards His chosen and righteous people, but He is just to impious sinners, and will render unto them according to their deeds and according to His clemency. His wrath, sent down upon the people, is felt in the impious king Napoleon, who has burned down many cities and villages. Napoleon has either killed the inhabitants or, having robbed them clean, has left them to suffer from cold and hunger, and to die from these torments. Even I was amidst that number and, as an impious transgressor, was punished by the merciful and just God. Recalling what has happened I pronounce with humility these words of the holy Prophet David: *O Lord, it is good for me that thou hast humbled me,* and again, *With chastisement hath the Lord chastened me, but He hath not given me over unto death* (Ps. 118:71, 117:18). Just imagine, being devoid of all attachments—how peaceful, how pleasant it became in my heart! I don't watch my trunk, it's been left for the worms to eat, and there is nothing for thieves to steal. Everywhere cleanliness is established and now it's absolutely calm. I am worried only about the fact that this is already the fifth month that I am living without any sort of occupation. My deepest bow bears witness [of my love] to you. I need your prayers and your blessings. I remain, wishing you every good thing, your sincere brother, sinful Alexander Putilov. January 11th, 1813.

✌ LETTER THREE ✌

My most kind Batiushka, Father Timothy!

Bless!

After my lengthy sorrow concerning you, finally, thanks be to God, I was overjoyed yesterday to receive a letter from you, the contents of which were so touching to my pained soul that I cannot worthily express without tears the pleasure that I felt then. Imagine how much I worried, tormented myself, and waited yesterday—and all that was in vain. I wanted to send an inquiry to the Briansk post office to see if my letter had been delivered to Fr. S.; but, glory be to God, you consoled me. Now I am at peace, but not entirely free. Beg God that He, through His ineffable goodness towards His creation, would *lead my soul out of prison* to repentance (Ps. 141:10). I have noticed that you are apparently worried that I have again become attached to the pernicious interests of the wicked world. Believe truly that which I have told you, that I for more than three months have not sought them, but have kept calmly to love towards God. But I must complain to you that they themselves do not leave of their own accord, and I find myself forced to drive them away, shielding myself with the protection of the Cross. You have convinced me, Batiushka, not to refrain from conversing with you; and therefore, entrusting my heart to the most sweet Redeemer Jesus, I am replying to your question, "When and to where?" as if before the tribunal of the Knower of hearts Himself. Without regret or duplicity, having called God's goodness to my aid, I have made up my mind to begin this previously commenced God-pleasing action on the first of next month: 1) to send my old [passport] to Moscow at the end of this month, in order to receive a new one and, when I receive it, to place it closer to my heart; 2) in the middle of that month, I will request a leave of absence of one week, or not more than a week and a half, on a praiseworthy pretext of certain circumstances that have arisen; I will propose this courteously; and finally, 3)if all of this has no effect, I will take up a spirit of tempest and wrath, and then, no manner of beast *shall be able to separate me from the love of God* (Romans 8:39), for which I give you as my witness the Master Most High. Now I have given you to understand "When?" In so doing, I will also inform you "To where?" You, Batiushka, have not at all let me know your own feelings, but have advised me to heed the inner urge and inclination of my soul, which has indicated to me the way and the place where you, in the beginning, were yourself inclined. In that very place I wish to make ready my way before God. However, I have made no previous announcement there, intending rather to simply show up without being expected. I don't know if I have thought this out well. And so, Batiushka, here I have told you all that you wanted to find out. Now I am letting you know that I am setting out upon this salvific path with full faith and hope in the Providence of the All-good God, and in your fatherly care and protection. I feel in full measure those words of yours, which you expressed to me, that you have the opportunity and the people to make the impossible possible. I am basing myself on this very word of yours, and without duplicity am stepping towards the beginning of all sorrows, for which I have already prepared myself, being assured that the words of Christ must come true for me as they did for you: *A man's fiercest foes shall be they of his own household* (cf. Matt: 10:36), whom, I feel in advance, the enemy of our common salvation, the devil, will set up against me. Imagine, kind Batiushka, at the very beginning of my attempt on the path of salvation, how much the vicious enemy troubles my spirit, placing before me obstacles, pressing in from all sides in wicked pursuit. Even my hair stands on end from fright and I am unable to worthily describe it to you. What kind of gloomy despondency gnaws at my poor heart? And who will help me the sinner in such dangers, if not Thee, O All-good Jesus God? In such a troubled situation I am consoled by the writings of the holy hierarch of Christ, Demetrius [of Rostov]. This is such nourishment that no matter how much I have read, it is so full of flavor, so pleasant and beneficial that I have never tasted anything like it in my life. I am extremely sorry, kind Batiushka, that you had to be summoned, being located such a great distance from the city. Moreover, I have erred in that I did not explain well enough to you the reason for which I forced you to go to receive my letter. I had wanted to reward you, according to my strength, with that which you lack materially, since you abundantly help me with my spiritual insufficiencies. In this very case I feared to send you anything more than this, relying upon your love, that you would accept a little gift as sufficient.

In addition to this, I am informing you about a new obstacle, which recently became known. Our brother Basil Ivanovich has decided to become the husband of an honorable maiden. This matter has already been initiated and will soon come to pass. To be precise: the 8th of this month will be the day of their marriage in the city of Suzdal, and it is my unavoidable misfortune to have to go there as well. Try to fully imagine all the inconveniences: the 75-mile trip, the cares, all the changes of horses and all the worries. But, concerning our brother, glory be to God! On my account, I will speak those words of the Apostle Paul that nothing *shall be able to separate me from the love of God* (Romans 8:39). This news about the marriage I ask you to keep to yourself for a while. If you are going to write to me, then write two letters at once—one about the present matters, and the other speaking your mind about my silence. Only, if you like, write a little more angrily, not giving the impression that you know anything; and, placing them both in one envelope, send them to me registered; so that, in case of my absence from the known route, it can be returned again to you, since my letter to you with its return took nine weeks. But under no circumstances should you not send it to me. I am so afraid of bad consequences that I can't even tell you, because in 1808 I suffered very severely. And so I hope that you will act in this instance prudently. Not doubting this for a moment, I remain your most submissive son, having much love for you and your pious soul, calling myself as I previously did. Forgive me, Batiushka! I have written to you in haste, with greater feeling than you can see from this.

(Signed) You know who.... November 2, 1815.

On the subject of writing me, please keep to my guide-lines....

⌣ LETTER FOUR ⌣

Most kind Batiushka,
Father Timothy!

Your letter, sent on the 5th of December, I received in good condition with great pleasure on the 21st. In my heartfelt grief I call you none other than my good consoler. May God reward you abundantly in His Kingdom for your sincere encourage-ment to me. Glory to God in the highest! My affairs have taken on a better appearance. My employer has promised me that he would release me from my job in the cellar to go to Moscow on the 1st. I asked his permission to go there under the pretext of getting a blessing from my mother and brother to get married, which has given extreme joy to all; but conditions require the marriage to be in Rostov. This is good. My intention was to enter the same place where you received your start, but from your letter I see otherwise. The devil, together with the world, by his evil-doings towards me put in my way a terrible obstacle to our seeing each other and to obtaining what is needed. But I overcame this temptation—just barely—and decided first to meet with you, and at the earliest and most opportune convenience. Then I decided, in the first days of January, to buy a horse together with the necessary equipment, and to hurry, to run without looking back, as if from Herod's sword. And in order not to suffer any needs on the way, I will take with me the betrothed Osip; for the Mother of the Lord escaped to Egypt with Her betrothed, the righteous Joseph. Osip speaks to me like Peter: *Even though all will betray you, yet will not I* (Mark 14:29). However, no one knows my secret, and even to him [to Osip] will I not reveal it before reaching you. This is all beautiful, but there is one "hitch"—I have still not received my passport from Moscow. And now I am sitting betwixt fear and hope, and I am hoping that this problem can be resolved in the next few days. As soon as I bring all this to the desired conclusion, I will set out without the slightest delay. I beg you, Batiushka, until then to pray to the Lord that He, through His ineffable goodness towards us, would *bring my soul* and body *out of* noetic *prison, that I may* ever freely *confess* His most Holy *Name* (Ps.141:10). Well, I have explained to you everything necessary. Until the longed-for conclusion, I beg your fatherly patience not to acknowledge the receipt of this. I am entrusting myself to the Providence of the all-good and righteous God and to your fatherly love and care, for the correction of a wretched sinner, who from now on will remain your absolutely obedient and devoted brother. A[lexander].

I bow to the earth before you. The 28th of December, 1815.

3
Excerpts from the Diary of Father Anthony

For 1820, 1823 and 1824

Direct, O Lord God, everything that I do, read and write, everything that I think, say and try to understand, to the glory of Thy Holy Name, for from Thee have I received a good beginning and my every deed ends in Thee.

O God, be attentive unto helping me. O Lord, make haste to help me (Ps. 69:1). February, 1820.

March 5th

IN EXPLAINING my fear to the Elder [Father Moses], I was told that the demons do not even have authority over swine.

In reading the Life of St. Hesychius, I saw how the demons wanted to make him afraid, when he came to the desert, of being devoured by wild beasts or of being slain by brigands, but he said to them: "I have come because of the multitude of my sins, let me be devoured by wild beasts or slain by robbers." And in this way he put them to shame.

March 6th

During Matins the desire came to me to write, with a blessing, an abbreviated version of the Rite of Monastic Tonsure. This would serve as a daily reminder to myself in order to counteract my forgetfulness and, in case of any sins, to make me reproach myself and to facilitate confession before a priest. I received a blessing to do this.

The Elder reminded us in the evening to pray for a weak brother and, as an illustration, he said: "When someone suffers any kind of bodily illness, then in various ways we minister to such a one, we nurse and co-suffer with him in his illness. In like manner, if someone is ailing in soul, we must help him by prayer to God."

St. Demetrius of Rostov said: "Prayer without attentiveness is like a censer without charcoal and incense."

March 7th

During Matins the desire arose to ask the Elder to chastise me in some way for every sin for the following reasons: 1) that by present chastisement I might avoid future punishment; 2) that by it I might be preserved from such falls another time.

In the evening during dinner I heard that gluttony doesn't strengthen a man, but only paralyzes him, and is nothing other than deception.

March 13th

Drinking hot water I felt myself to be very much like one drunk. May the Lord deliver me from drinking this, by my [spiritual] father's prayers.

At the beginning of this month, while the Elder was explaining to us about the labor of fasting and the benefit of it, and about weakness, I heard that before God one prostration of a weak man is of no less worth than ten done without difficulty.

March 18th

After lunch the Elder spoke to the brethren about obedience. As an example, he said that the ministering spirits, that is, the angels, by nature are good, but they fulfill not their own will, but God's will. How much more ought we men to be found in obedience.

Because of an incident of my failure to grasp things, I was seized by despondency. I saw that only when I think poorly of myself am I found to have a true opinion about myself, but when I think well of myself, then I fall into delusion.

March 19th

St. John of the Ladder said: "Whoever in the beginning was not in obedience cannot have humility of wisdom."

March 21st

Brother Sabbas was clothed in the angelic habit and named Sabbatius. May the Lord strengthen him in the struggle that lies before him.

O God, be attentive unto helping me. O Lord, make haste to help me (Ps. 69:1).

Direct, O Lord God, everything that I do, read and write, everything that I think, say and try to understand, to the glory of Thy Holy Name, for from Thee have I received a good beginning and my every deed ends in Thee.

Grant me, O God, that I might not anger Thee, my Creator, in word, deed or thought, but may all my deeds, counsels and thoughts be to the glory of Thy most Holy Name!

1823

December 1st

In this little book, abandoned by me out of laziness for a fourth year, I have again from this day begun to write with the blessing of Fr. Moses, putting in it what is beneficial and necessary for my notice. Bless, O Lord!

Out of self-will, I made for myself a prayer rope out of string without the blessing of the Elder and, seeing my mistake, I threw it into the stove as a demonic work. A thought said to me at the time: although you began a good deed by your own will, without the counsel and blessing of the Elder, consider it all a demonic activity.

December 2nd

I prepared today to serve and receive the Mysteries of Christ, but because of my shameless pride and cunning in confession of sins, I was not allowed by my Elder to serve until I have cleansed my conscience by true confession without concealing my sins from him. Having confessed before him everything pure-heartedly with humility, I expected for myself a bitter chastisement for my cunning, but the words of St. David came to pass in me: *"The righteous man shall chasten me with mercy* (Ps.140:6). For he was very meek and, commiserating with me, he reprimanded me. In conclusion, he ordered me to write on my heart for permanent remembrance and implementation the following eight points: 1) to renounce my own understanding and will; 2) in meeting each person to place myself lower than him no matter where we meet; 3) to root the remembrance of death deeper in the heart; 4) self-reproach; 5) to always have humble prayer; 6) to bear reproach, whenever it arises from someone, with joy as spiritual medicine; 7) to carry out precisely whatever I am told; 8) if it happens that out of forgetfulness or habit I sin again in some way, to confess it pure-heartedly, as it is, without cunning. And I asked Batiushka with tears that he would entreat God that I might treasure above all the last of the eight points that he told me, that is, pure-hearted confession, for I have almost never had it throughout my whole life. He promised in turn to lay on me a penance for my sins, whatever penance the Lord might reveal to him, for the sake of my chastity and the propitiation of God's righteousness.

December 5th

After the sixth ode [at Matins], the Life of St. Zachariah the son of Karion was read. When he wanted to die, he was questioned by St. Moses about what he saw. He replied: "Is there anything better than to keep silent, father?" "Yea, child, be silent." Then the thought came to me to reply in such a manner to Brother Gregory in order to counter his empty questions: "Is there anything better for us, Brother Gregory, than to be silent?"

After Liturgy I asked Fr. Methodius about prayer, telling him that I live very badly, and he said to me: "One must have a contrite heart."

In the evening, revealing my thoughts to the Elder, I said that Fr. Methodius had asked me in church which image [icon] is better painted. And the Elder told me this: "That image [mode of life] is better which keeps silent," relating this to the living image, man, who treasures silence, not being curious about anything.

December 6th

Having read the prayer-rule for Holy Communion after Matins, I went to the Elder to confess my sins. From long-standing habit, at confession I always conceal my wicked actions. He said to me concerning this: "The bodily eye cannot tolerate even the smallest speck of dust on its surface, so too the conscience, when soiled by something, cannot attain prayer."

A week ago Batiushka gave me a commandment: not to be curious about anything, neither to listen to the empty conversations of others, humbly saying to them that I don't have a blessing from the Elder to do this.

December 13th

St. John Chrysostom said: "As fire is to gold, so is affliction for the soul, washing away defilement, making one pure, clear and radiant, this leads to the Kingdom." For this reason, too, Christ said, *In the world ye shall have tribulation* (John 16:33) as something that brings one great good.

A thought came to me: the Saviour commanded us to forgive our brother his sins seventy times seven in a day; but you, wretched one, don't even want to forgive him once.

Having confessed my grief at a brother to Batiushka, I was told: "We must bear nobly others' infirmities of soul without grievance. Therefore, if someone is ill in body, we not only do not become distressed at him, but moreover we serve him in every way. In such a manner one must address maladies of the soul.

December 14th

I remarked to Batiushka that I was embittered in regards to bearing the infirmities of the brothers and trusting in their improvement for the better. In conclusion he told me: "No matter in what filthy situation you happen to see someone, you must not be surprised nor doubt the possibility of his improvement, for many drunkards have finally become sober, the unruly meek, fornicators chaste, and so forth. And St. John Chrysostom said, 'You should doubt only about the amendment of him who is in hell with the demons.'"

December 19th

A conversation took place with Fr. Israel about the typicon, that one must conform to it in everything (concerning prostrations), but a thought said to me at the same time, that one must expend more effort about one's moral character than about the typicon.

December 25th

In the morning after confession Batiushka gave me three commandments to keep: 1) simplicity of heart; and the other two a demon stole from me that very hour through forgetfulness, for at the time I could not write them down.

December 29th

Batiushka blessed me to drink hot water on the Feast of the Nativity of Christ to the glory of God, but I, by the action of a demon in me, thought to refrain from it, in violation of the vow I had given to carry out exactly everything I had been commanded, and from this violation I felt great despondency. A thought at the time, upbraiding me for formulating my own understanding, said: "Even if Batiushka were to bless you to eat meat, or to try some carcass, then it would be far better and more beneficial than your self-styled continence." O Lord, grant me, through my father's prayers, to do everything he commands me without deliberation!

December 30th

In the evening I explained to Batiushka that my brothers' shortcomings involuntarily bring distress to my heart. And in reply to this I heard from him: "I bear all your shortcomings with magnanimity, and I am not surprised at any of your infirmities. If I were to become grieved in my position [as Abbot] and demand a strict account from each brother, then I would have exploded long ago."

December 31st

Today after Matins, by my own experience, I saw how in adverse circumstances, in reproachful reprimands, derision, strict inquiries, whether just or unjust, there is nothing better than humility with a bow: for he who humbles himself, the same will receive consolation in spirit; he who exalts himself, he will afterwards have to endure unbearable grief from his conscience. Thus, for a monk humility is a victory, while defeat is obstinacy and stubbornness. Grant me, O Lord, for the sake of my [spiritual] father's prayers, to follow what is beneficial.

1824

January 9th

For three days in a row I have been enduring a great diabolic temptation of despondency, sloth and heedlessness. At the time I was totally without restraint; I spoke idly with everyone as much as I liked. In the evening, having come to the cell of Brother Gregory without any need, I inclined to idle-talking and served as an obstacle to his work in his cell. Among other things I told him: I want to have a drink now, but the Elder is not here and I dare not do so without a blessing. But he said to me: "Father, it's better to have a drink without a blessing than to talk idly."

Informing Batiushka about my idle-talking and about unnecessary questions, I heard from him: "If you ask what is not needed, you will hear what is not needed."

Uglich—The Transfiguration Cathedral and
Bell Tower in the Kremlin.

January 11th

Batiushka assigned me and all the younger brothers a penance: whichever one of us, during a common occupation, is the first to speak idly, as a punishment for failing to restrain his tongue, he is to make five prostrations and ask everyone's forgiveness.

January 27th

During Matins a thought, reproaching me for drinking unrestrainedly, said, "Too much of anything is harmful."

February 6th

Batiushka sent a brother to me, asking me to set aside my work and go quickly to Vespers. I wanted to finish the task, and by that act I extremely grieved Batiushka, so that he became ashamed. I expected a severe rebuke and penance for my disobedience, but in its place I received a meek reprimand and, what is more, an apple as a consolation. O Lord, protect me from similar demonic villainy, through the prayers of my spiritual father!

ОПТИНА ПУСТЫНЬ.
Внутренный видъ Св.
вороть Предтеченскаго
скита

Inside view of the Holy Gates of the St. John the Forerunner Skete.

4

An Excerpt from the Personal Calendar of Abbot Anthony

In 1842, before Vespers on Sunday, May 17th, His Eminence Philaret, Metropolitan of Kiev, on his trip from St. Petersburg to Kiev favored us with a visit at the Maloyaroslavets St. Nicholas Monastery. With all the brethren entrusted to me, I met him at the holy gates with the Holy Cross, to the ringing of bells and the singing of the troparion [to St. Nicholas]: "The truth of things hath revealed thee to thy flock...." The Bishop spent the night in the superior's quarters and kindly conversed with me on various subjects. I dared to explain to him about my unworthiness to direct the monastery and my feeblemindedness, but he replied with a smile: "What is to be done? Even if you're not too bright, you're still the Abbot!"

The next day, early in the morning of the 18th, Vladika wished to go to Kaluga, where I, with his blessing, accompanied him. We arrived at Kaluga after Liturgy, at 12 noon, and he was met by our Bishop about two miles from the city. At the St. Laurence Monastery he was ceremoniously met at the holy gates with the Holy Cross by the brethren of the archiepiscopal residence, by the honored clergy, the members of the Consistory and a choir of singers. In the church there was a litany and the singing to him of "Many Years." He stayed in the cells of our

Bishop, and on the following day, the 19th, set out for the Kaluga Cathedral, where he was also ceremoniously met at the doors, and was greeted with a speech by the cathedral archpriest. He served the Liturgy with our Bishop in the Cathedral. For the first time in my life, I was vouchsafed to see such a solemn service with two hierarchs.

After the celebration of the Liturgy, His Eminence deigned to visit the Kaluga Theological Seminary, and from there the St. Laurence Monastery, where our Bishop had prepared a banquet for the great visitor and had invited many to it—not only clergymen, but also municipal officials, such as the provincial governor, the marshal of the nobility, the chairman of all the legislatures, and several of the prominent citizens. I, too, the unworthy one, was favored with an invitation to the meal, and thought to sit in the last place, lower than everyone. But it turned out otherwise—that is, I wound up sitting opposite the Metropolitan himself, and having the consolation of hearing his edifying conversation with many individuals. He also deigned to speak a few remarkable words to me, which I will not write down here for the sake of brevity. During the meal the singers gave various recitals. At the beginning they sang "Our Father," and at the end, at the time of the toasts, "Many Years." After the meal, thanking the host and guests for the bread and salt, all departed.

It was entrusted to me from both bishops to set out for Optina Monastery with the news that the Kievan Metropolitan intended to visit the holy Monastery. I set out for there that same evening, travelled at night, and arrived in Optina towards morning on the 20th. Vladika himself arrived that very day toward evening, and was ceremoniously met by the Superior and a multitude of his brethren at the holy gates with the Holy Cross. After entering the church and blessing everyone, he himself deigned to serve a panikhida for our Elder, Fr. Leonid, and for the honored citizen and benefactor of the Monastery and Skete, Demetrius Vasilievich Bruzgin.

After this, Vladika blessed me to go to the Skete with his cell-attendant Callistus and his house-secretary, and to guide them there through all the places of interest. We arrived there in the evening. I first showed them the holy skete church and the adjacent bishop's cells. I told them, and indicated with my hand, who lives where. Then we walked around inside the Skete, around the entire enclosure. Having passed through the Skete, I went up first onto the footbridge that is located alongside the garden nursery. Suddenly I was overtaken by an unexpectedly grievous trial—a wide piece of the bridge broke under me and I fell below, dislocating my right arm at the shoulder. In a split second there arose unbearable pain and the arm began to swell up, so that even my heart began to hurt. Groaning, I was barely able to drag myself to the nearest cell, where I collapsed and spent the entire night without sleep in grievous sufferings, about which Vladika was notified. He came and visited me, the sufferer, at night and with pity asked: "What happened to you?" and he promised to implore the wonderworkers of Kiev for my healing. On the morning of the 21st a bone specialist was brought to me. Twice he set about to correct it, but it didn't work; and finally, the third time, the arm barely fell back into place. What terrible pain I felt during the straightening out of my arm I am unable to describe. Finally my arm was bound so that I would not endanger it again while it was still not strengthened in its place. I even had to cross myself with my left hand, and to take food and fulfill other needs with that hand as well. I saw then by experience what a great blessing from God to man is the right hand, and I had perceived this earlier. But for all this, I thanked the Lord God from the bottom of my soul, that I, by my fall and the dislocation of my arm, preserved others from a similar trial, since the Kievan Metropolitan himself intended to pass through the Skete at that same spot. And if I had not preserved him by my own fall from such a severe trial, there would have been a thousand times more grief. But the Lord God had detained him in the Monastery at that point, and one might say, *Wondrous is God in His saints!* (Ps. 67:35). And for me, the sinner, to whom this happened, this trial has remained as a lesson for my whole life: so that I would move my feet with the fear of God.

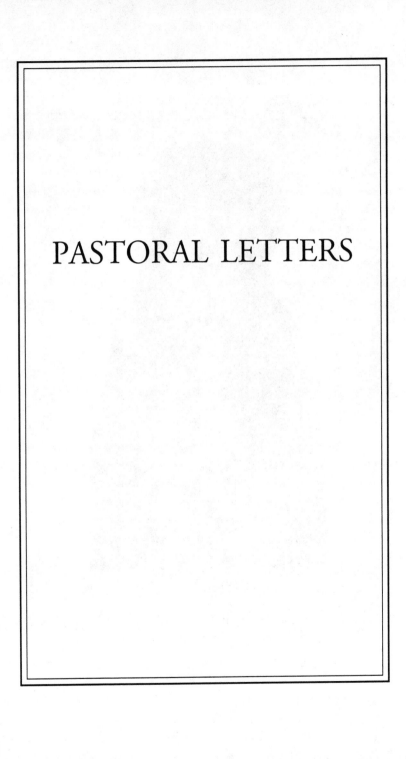

PASTORAL LETTERS

Icon of St. Anthony, Elder of Optina, painted by N. A. Papkov
for the glorification of all the Optina Saints in 1991.

Selected Pastoral Letters
of Elder Anthony

ON POVERTY
Letter 99*

Seeing your letters about the poor health of your entire family as well as about your family needs and lack of finances, I sorrow in heart. What can be done? What happens to us happens not without God's allowance, as the Righteous Job said: as the Lord wills, so may it be. Therefore like him, you must courageously endure everything unpleasant that happens in life and refrain from murmuring and say not, "Why is it like this and not like that?" For as St. Isaac the Syrian says, "You are not wiser than God; and do not sorrow when you are not heard by Him."** For if the Lord wants to take your cherished son to Himself, even then you cannot reproach Him that He might take to Himself what is His, but with obedience you should say, "Our Heavenly Father, may Thy holy will concerning us be done in everything!" By this, that is, by your obedience, it will be easier for you to bear your deprivation. To this end I deeply co-suffer with you over your monetary poverty and I think that this temptation might simply be to test you, since when formerly

---

* Believed to have been written to Simeon I. Yanovsky, disciple of St. Herman of Alaska.

** Homily Three, p. 24.

you had money in abundance, you did not know its value, and roubles flowed forth from your little pocket as if they were worthless kopeks; but presently one pocket has become empty and there isn't anything in the other. Therefore, endure the grief of poverty and drink water in place of honey mead. Then again do not be disturbed. For the Lord God, rich in mercy and compassion, will not leave you without His clemency. Cast your care upon Him and He will nourish you. St. David says: *All the men of wealth have slept their sleep and have found nothing in their hands* (Ps. 75:6). Recently I beheld in a dream at night: I had prepared to dispatch to you 3,000 roubles, and I was writing to you to use them to build your new house and to send me an account of the building project. But having awakened I did not find any riches in my hand; however, I rejoiced in that even in my sleep I did not abandon my care for you.

June 25th, 1855.

THE MEDICINE OF LIFE
Letter 110

With my whole heart I sympathize with you over your beloved sister's acute and prolonged illness. I am entreating the Lord God for her, that He might renew her feeble strength to nobly bear her sufferings (because impatience will bring her no relief), and that He might lighten them. From her acute illness she may conclude that the Lord God loves her as His bride more than all your sisters. When she nobly bears her sufferings, then the Lord Himself abides with her invisibly as He said by the mouth of St. David: *I am with him in affliction, and I will rescue him and glorify him. With length of days will I satisfy him, and I will show him My salvation* (Ps. 90:15-16). See how fortunate your sister is! I advise her to strengthen herself in her affliction by Communion of the Holy Mysteries of Christ and to read in the book *A Day of Holy Life* by Bishop Gregory of Kazan the article "How to Conduct Oneself in Time of Illness." This book, if you don't have it, may be requested from any book store; it is not expensive, is cheaper than medication from a pharmacy and more beneficial.

I, by God's great mercy to my unworthiness, have had open sores on my legs for 25 years, but I do not suffer in the way that the righteous Lazarus suffered who had neither shelter, nor servants, nor medication, nor food or drink and had no one to console him besides the dogs. But I, the wicked one, have peaceful and comfortable cells, a zealous assistant, a doctor and medication, and kind visitors without number, and as much food and drink as my stomach can possibly digest. Thus, I don't suffer quite as much as I am cared for. Woe unto me the wicked one!

February 18th, 1861.

THE AFFLICTIONS OF CHILDREN
Letter 116

Hearing that your family's holy habitation has not been free from sickness nor from certain disturbances, I pity you in my heart and have asked the Lord God as far as I am able that He would visit and heal your infirmities for His name's sake. What is to be done? The Lord has so disposed that our temporal life should not be without sorrows, as it is said: every head is in pain and every heart in sorrow. But most astonishing of all is that not a single holy man, no matter how holy and perfect he may have been, has lived his life without enduring some hardship, so that he might not exalt himself. And if the saints suffered adversity, how much more should we endure!

The painful sufferings of your innocent and angelic B. have also greatly pained my heart. I have asked the Lord that for your consolation He preserve his life and lighten his affliction. For I know that although all children are dear to their parents' hearts, the littlest make the greatest claim. I will not hide from you that from the depths of my soul I love all your God-beloved children, but B., as my favorite, I love more, and remember him more often. I ask you to tell him this for me. I also ask you to tell him the news that the birds have begun to fly to our monastery forest from different locales, and sing each morning for several hours. And today a cuckoo bird cuckooed three times. They are all waiting for the sweet-singing nightingale to form a choir and propose to sing a fine concert upon B's arrival: *Praise the Lord all ye winged birds,* and *elders with the younger let them praise the name of the Lord* (Ps. 148:7,10,12). However, I don't know if you will be able to free yourself this summer to come to us. For there is the civil service, domestic tasks, the long journey and its expense. And the most important consideration is that the fullness of consolation that you tasted in the presence of our God-beloved Elder Fr. Macarius will not be present. But to see those places in which he lived might be bitter, for the joy of love can be tearful. For this reason may the Lord grant you a good thought, that you would do the right thing. I also ask you to forgive my feeble-mindedness for talking about the birds to your God-beloved B. in the language of a child.

April 1st, 1864.

VISION OF GOD
Letter 121

I advise you to receive Communion of the Holy Mysteries in all the holy fasts. Besides this, if some illness happens to befall you, don't send for a doctor or an apothecary, but for a priest of God and ask him to confess you and give you Holy Communion. Only then should you send for medicine, for it is more exceedingly salvific to feed the soul with Incorruptible and Holy Bread. If a person were to die on a day on which he had received Communion of the Holy Mysteries, then the holy Angels would receive his soul in their arms in honor of the Communion, and he would pass through all the aerial toll-houses* unscathed.

September 15th, 1859.

P.S. I feel for your sister since she is deprived of sight in one eye. I also am able to use only one eye, but I can gaze upon God. Thus, advise your sister from me that with her eye that is clear she gaze at heaven and with the other at the vanity of vanities so that she does not see them.

AFFLICTION AND THE WILL OF GOD
Letter 124

To my Most Honorable and Kind Benefactress and Much-suffering Slave of Christ, N.

Be strong in the Lord!

Your greatly ailing and comfortless state of health causes my heart to grieve with you. Because of my duty of love and compassion, I have prayed for you daily and entreat the Lord God that He grant you Christian patience in your illness, and alleviation. But if your illness continues to the present time, this is not because God has not heard the prayers that have been offered to Him, but because He leaves certain ones without healing so as to more readily benefit the sufferer. Through temporal suffering a sinful man not only is freed from eternal torments for his sins, but is also granted salvation and made an heir of the Heavenly Kingdom. The Lord God in His profound

---

* For more information on the "aerial toll-houses," see *The Soul After Death* by Fr. Seraphim Rose (St. Herman of Alaska Brotherhood, 1980).

wisdom truly arranges all things through His love for mankind and grants to everyone that which is profitable. It is our duty not to question why something happens this way and not that, but with childlike submissiveness to devote ourselves to the holy will of our heavenly Father and say from the depths of our soul: Holy Father, Thy will be done! With this in mind, if one looks at a healthy man and looks at a man who has suffered long, and observes the state of soul of the one and the other, then which one of them can be called blessed or accursed—the healthy man or the suffering man? For example, how many times during your illness have you brought repentance for your sins before the Lord God and before your spiritual father and received Communion of the Holy Mysteries? Meanwhile, the healthy man rarely thinks about his sins; and if he happens to make preparation for Communion once a year, it is due not so much to his fervency as to propriety, so that he may say: "I have confessed and received Communion." But his confession would be like that of a dumb man, that is, it would seem that there was nothing weighing on his soul. How many times have you in your illness heaved heavy sighs from the depths of your soul before God, every one of which the Lord sees and hears? But with the healthy it is not at all this way. If they sigh, it is usually because they haven't seen someone for a long time or because it has been long since they have received news about something. In your illness you have often moistened your face with your tears, but healthy people waste soap on their face daily instead of using tears to clean it, and not a word is mentioned about the soul. In your illness you have often turned your eyes with prayer to the icon of Christ the Saviour and to His Most Pure Mother, but healthy ladies or girls, instead of gazing at an icon, look a hundred times a day at themselves in the mirror, and rarely pray hard or cross themselves as they should. For these reasons you are more blessed in your ailing condition than all the healthy ones around you. Furthermore, eternal blessedness in the heavens has been prepared for you by the Lord God, about which in your suffering you should rejoice and be glad and from your whole soul thank the merciful God. For a great multitude of mercies and consolations have been prepared for those who suffer, which mercies you too will in time receive, at the prayers of the Theotokos.

At this point, for your information, I will tell you about your beloved child A. B. Thanks be to the Lord God, she is healthy and safely walks the saving path! Rejoice at this and thank the Lord God that He has called your child to His service. May God grant that your other children would have the same concern for the salvation of their souls; for may God have mercy on us if we should neglect our souls. As our body contracts various infirmities, so does our soul. There is bodily blindness and there is a blindness of the soul. Some people have dark water that clouds the eyes, and although they look, they can't see anything. Similarly there can also be a murky water in the eyes of the soul, which also obscures vision. And if that person comes to the abyss of evil, he doesn't see it and doesn't do anything about the salvation of his soul. For this reason the Holy Fathers have directed us to pray daily to Christ our Saviour, crying to Him: *Enlighten mine eyes*, O Christ God, *lest at any time I sleep unto death. Lest at any time mine enemy say I have prevailed against him* (Ps. 12:3-4).

No date

THE JUDGMENT
Letter 133

May the Lord God console you who weep, may He calm your grieving heart with good hope!

Your announcement about the repose of your dearest father moved my heart to grieve with you for him and even more so over you. You and I, according to the Apostle's word, *have many instructors in Christ, yet have ... not many fathers* (I Cor.4:15). Thus, having lost a child-loving father, it would not be praiseworthy if one did not moisten one's face with tears, which often serve as an expression of love: but it must not be beyond measure or it would be a sin. If I may be permitted, I should say in all fairness that one should weep not so much over the dead as over oneself, as Christ the Saviour said to the women weeping over Him: *O Daughters of Jerusalem! Weep not for Me, but weep for yourselves!* (Luke 23:28). That which makes you sorrowful, that your father met the end of his life, as it were, without a Christian departure, is really not known to us. Perhaps his death happened martyrically; such a death transcends the last rites [of the Church]. It is well known that St. Athanasius of Mount Athos was killed by the collapse of the church edifice, but his soul dwells among good things with the Lord. Many die at present from thunderclaps, lightning, from fire, from water, from asphyxiation, from unfortunate falls and so forth, and such deaths are martyric, in that the sins of these people are cleansed by their own blood. Our holy Church makes special intercession for such ones before the Lord. For this reason be at peace, Matushka, and do not consider your father's death to be unfortunate, since the judgments of God are unfathomable to us sinners. For the Lord God "by the depths of His wisdom orders all things in His love for mankind and grants unto all that which is profitable" (Troparion for Saturday). We out of our lack of understanding regard certain aspects of someone's death to be dishonorable, but that person will ultimately appear amidst the number of the sons of God, that is, the righteous. Thus our Elder Father G. was alive, joyful and healthy and then suddenly his days came to an end. Truly, *as for man, his days are as the grass; as a flower of the field so shall he blossom forth* (Ps. 102: 13).

I have written down the name of your dearest father for annual commemoration on our list and he will be remembered daily at the *proskomedia,* Liturgies, *litia* and the reading of the Psalter. I myself served the first panikhida together with other priests. May the Lord God forgive him his sins voluntary and involuntary and grant his soul rest with the saints in the Heavenly Kingdom and may He by His mercy console you who weep, are in affliction and wait for the consolation of Christ.

January 10th, 1843.

CONSOLATION FROM BEYOND THE GRAVE
Letter 142

With great sorrow in my soul I will tell you about a terrible calamity which took place in our monastery barn, the likes of which I have never seen during my 42 years here, and may God grant that such a thing never happen again. On the morning of March 1st, one maiden Nadezhda, pouring hot water from a cauldron to wash dirty laundry, stumbled and fell into the cauldron, and burned herself horribly in the boiling water. But thanks be to the Lord God, she lived two more days, in full consciousness, and, being provided the sacraments [of Confession, Unction and Holy Communion], quietly reposed on Sunday at three o'clock. Hearing of this horrible occurrence, I wept bitterly, and even until now I can't think about it without becoming distressed. I mentally reproach myself that although I have personally suffered from an affliction of my legs for 26 years, nonetheless my affliction isn't even worth mentioning in comparison with the suffering which the maiden Nadezhda endured before her death, but rather it is like enduring spitting or bruises. The Great-martyr Nadezhda* endured her horrible suffering without a cry or shout, while I live in plenty and eat everything in sight.

I will add one wonderful occurrence to this. The same day that this happened Father M. returned to his cell from Matins and, having lain down and fallen asleep, he saw in a deep sleep Father Archimandrite Moses directing him (Father M.) to hurry immediately to the barn where he was needed right away. Awakening at once, Father M. raced to the barn in amazement and there encountered the grievous news. From this you can conclude that Batiushka Archimandrite Moses, even after his repose, vigilantly cares for everything in our monastery, for which may we give glory to God.

March 9th, 1863.

P.S. I will tell you something else about Archimandrite Moses. Before the burial of the maiden Nadezhda, one young woman (a milkmaid) in a deep sleep saw the Archimandrite in a mantle walking to church with a staff where the newly-reposed had been carried. Receiving a blessing, she asked: "Where are you hurrying to Batiushka?" He replied: "To see Nadezhda off." Thus you see what consoling dreams about my holy father come to pass.

DISCERNING THE CALL TO THE MONASTIC LIFE
Letter 145

By your letter you have revealed to me the desire which has been born in your heart to dedicate yourself to the service of God in the monastic calling. But your parents trouble them-selves to betroth you in marriage, and hence you are perplexed in deciding what to do. To this I will say that the married life is a life blessed by God, and the monastic life is a holy and angelic

---

* In English, the name Nadezhda translates as "Hope."

life. Both ways of life are pleasing to God. But in the married life how often does one meet with various concerns and grief? And so the ancient proverb puts it fairly: the farther you are from the sea, the less the grief. About the monastic path one can say this: that it is a blessed life; however, it is not an easy one, but one full of toil. Therefore, if one can say concerning tailoring that one must measure seven times and cut but once, then one must first consider monastery life not seven times, but seventy times, and then, once and for all, resolve to enter the holy monastic life in the monastery. If you are now impatient, drowsy, lazy toward prayer, intemperate and disinclined to work, etc., if you are sometimes not without vexations when listening to remarks from your parents, rebukes, refusals of your requests, and so forth, then in the monastery it will be even more difficult, for there, until the grave, one's entire life is spent in toil, labors, in submission and in setting aside one's will and desires. One must obey not only the Abbess, but also the eldresses and sisters in Christ, and the lady must become a maidservant, that is, an unquestioning, all-submissive servant until her final breath. Therefore, you yourself must deliberate whether or not you will have enough strength and courage to bear such labors. In addition, look at your sister who, after four years of monastery life, has become a decrepit and sick old woman due to extreme fasting and labors. Ask her whether life in the monastery is easy or not. Will she approve of your intention to live with her? So it appears to me that married life will be more tolerable for you than life in the monastery. I am not telling you this with the goal of discouraging you from Mary's better part, the monastic life, and of praising the way of Martha (Luke 10:38-42), the wedded life of much turmoil, but so that you, like a wise virgin, would not think about this matter light-mindedly. Ask the Lord God in fervent prayer for an understanding of this, saying, "O Lord, grant me a good

ELDER ANTHONY OF OPTINA

thought. O Lord, teach me to do what is right. O Lord, arrange my life according to Thy holy will, and not according to mine. Our Father, Thy will be done."

I ask that the Lord God may grant you understanding, His aid and blessing in every good thing.

February 9th, 1857.

LOVE FOR THE WORLD AND LOVE FOR GOD
Letter 164

Your Godliness, all-honorable and most respected friend and benefactor in Christ the Saviour!

May you be healthy in body and soul and rejoice in the Sweetest Saviour Christ, Who has called you to His service!

Not having received a letter from you for a long time, I had already begun to consider that perhaps I might have hurt you by my last letter. But when I read what you wrote, I was exceedingly consoled: first, because of your good disposition toward my unworthiness, and secondly because I saw from your letter your great love for Christ the Saviour and the call from Him to serve Him in the ranks of the angels though clothed in flesh. For this cause I rejoice in my heart and from my whole soul I thank the Lord God Who has placed in you the desire to acquire the eternal salvation of your soul. I entreat His Great Goodness to lift you up and perfect your desire while the flame of your love for Him has not been extinguished.

Having read your letter through, I noticed in it much that was similar to my former situation; for, undertaking to leave the world for the sake of God, I too felt, while I was in the world, a prolonged despondency, fear and perplexity. Love for my aged mother kept me in the world, as well as love for my brothers, for my sisters, love for my relatives, love for my friends, and love of money. It was as if my heart was bound by some kind of iron chain. But the frequent remembrance of the unknown hour of death broke these *bonds asunder,* and my *soul like a sparrow was delivered out of the snare of the hunters.* The snare is broken by the remembrance of death, and by God's goodness I was delivered (Ps. 115:7, 123:6-7). So you, too, my beloved friend, can overcome similar obstacles by the remembrance of death. Of course, the law of nature and the command of God obliges us to honor and love our parents. But St. John of Damascus in a church hymn says: "As a man has a tender feeling for his mother, so much warmer should be our love towards the Lord." (Hymns of Ascent, Sunday, tone 4). If one loves his parents more than he should, Christ the Saviour Himself speaks to such a one: *He is not worthy of me* (Matthew 10:37). Perhaps this further thought also disturbs you: "Who will look after my mother in her old age?" In this case you should mentally ask yourself: "If the scythe of death should, for my sins, cut me down before my parents, who would take care of my mother in her old age? Who would watch over my sister's peace and other matters? Who?" Unfailingly an inner voice will reply to this troubling question: "No one, except God." So also, if someone should leave their parents for God's sake before their own death, or should parents leave their children, then the Lord God takes those left behind under His special care and Providence. This contemplation should console that person, that having abandoned his family he has placed God in his former position as care-giver.

Concerning your father's request that you not avoid your assignment in the civil service, you should consider such praise-worthy advice of your father as holy and follow it, but only if you have consigned yourself once and for all to life in the world. One must prefer God's calling above all advice, according to the word of St. David: *Today if ye will hear His voice, harden not your hearts* (Ps. 94:8). For our Lord is so full of love for mankind and so merciful to our unworthiness, that He wills that all be saved and come to a knowledge of the truth, and calls everyone to the heavenly supper to reign together with Him, which reign will have no end. But those called were so foolish and so ungrateful that, as each one engaged himself in some affair, He began to reject them all. They were all busy for one or another reason, and had some excuse to refuse, such as taking a wife, possessing a village, buying a yoke of oxen (cf. Luke 14:16-19). You, my beloved, have neither wife, nor village, nor oxen. You are still free; therefore you have no reasons to excuse yourself, for you should, according to the word of St. Symeon the New Theologian, "have no desire to keep the slightest attachment to this world, not even for good motives, for in fact they would only be silly pretenses. When you have been called, obey instantly, for nothing pleases God so much as our swift response" (Read about this in the Philokalia, part 1, leaf 44 obverse, chapters 9,10 and 11.)* The word "called" refers to being called to God; for He alone enlightens mankind, grants him understanding and calls him to the path of salvation. (He either mystically enlightens and reveals His will directly by His grace, or He gives us understanding through the reading of the Divine Scriptures. He has a grace-filled effect upon the heart of man, and by many other ways mysterious and unfathomable to us calls us to the path of salvation.) Do not think that by this I am giving you a firm direction to abandon the world. I dare not attempt to persuade anyone to enter the monastic life, for I know that the Lord God does not abide in monasteries alone, but His grace is present in every place and His dominion is in every generation and generation, as the holy David affirms, saying: *If I go up into heaven, Thou art there; if I go down into*

---

* Found in Symeon the New Theologian, *The Practical and Theological Chapters,* trans. Paul McGuckin (Kalamazoo, Michigan: Cistercian Publications, 1982), pp. 37-38.

hades, Thou art present there. If I take up my wings toward the dawn, and make mine abode in the uttermost parts of the sea, even there shall Thy hand guide me (Ps. 138:7-9). And so, beloved, I wish most fervently, and in the name of God I implore that you would obey above all the inner conviction of your conscience, and by her counsel choose for yourself what is best and most profitable. Nonetheless, even if my words are not opposed to God's will, I suggest in any case that you at your discretion follow them or leave them. Your letter and my heartfelt love for you prompted me to write so much to you, for which I ask forgiveness.

Very sinful Hieromonk Anthony

September 8th, 1832.

A SPIRITUAL GUIDE
Letter 180

Thanks be to the Lord God that a pleasant summer is approaching you, in which after the manner of Israel of old one must leave the works of Pharaoh, that is, the cares of the world, flee from Egypt and head for the Promised Land flowing with honey and the milk of spiritual consolations which, not as much in this world as in the next, are prepared by God for those who fervently serve Him. Hence, just as those who went out from Egypt had Moses as their guide, and those fleeing from Sodom had an angel as their instructor, so you, in the words of St. John Climacus, must have a Moses interceding for you before God and serving as your instructor. Whoever trusts his own understanding and thinks that he has no need of an instructor will soon stray from the straight path. Therefore, you must entreat the Lord God with tears to grant you an unerring instructor or instructress; for an experienced and skilled physician needed according to the putridity of the disease. One must therefore seek not for a peaceful and well-equipped hospital so much as for a skilled physician.

You have told me that you need to speak about the past or what transpired at a certain time. Yes, this is necessary, for everything manifest is light, and light disperses the darkness, that is, the devil with his foul suggestions and recollections. For this reason if a man does not carefully restrain himself, it is very unlikely that he will not stain himself in some way due to his youth. These stains cannot be removed so easily by any other means than spoken confession. Although the Lord God knows all our weaknesses, and foresees even things not yet done by us, and has no need to be told what is already known to Him, nonetheless, for our benefit He says or rather orders through the Prophet: *Declare thou* thy sins *that thou mayest be justified* (Is. 43:26). Thus, you will see how necessary spoken confession is for the remission of sins, for without it we cannot even lay a good beginning, nor be saved, nor have peace of soul. That is why it is necessary to reveal and examine what has taken place. I have not spoken about this so that I might be told these things, but so that you would tell what is needed to someone whom your soul particularly trusts. This is my counsel to you for your spiritual benefit. Nonetheless, all this is subject to your free will: you should do whatever is most profitable to you.

St. John of the Ladder counsels everyone who wants to enter the arena of the monastic calling to first come to the monastery as if one were merely visiting, to observe the monastery's order, and, to the extent possible, to test (as far as we are capable) the superior himself, whether instead of a captain we have chanced upon a simple sailor, or instead of a physician—a sick patient, or in place of the undefiled—the lascivious.* Relative to this,

---

* *The Ladder of Divine Ascent,* Step 4:6 (Brookline, Massachusetts: Holy Transfiguration Monastery, 1979), p. 22.

our reverend Mother N. asked me to tell you that you should come to visit them the first time without a time limit, although it may be until your death, and observe their manner of life, at the same time testing your own infirmity, and only then resolutely give yourself over once and for all to the service of the Lord God. It is in just such a manner that I set about at the beginning of my withdrawal from the world; at first I came to Fr. Moses not to live with him forever, but only to visit and take counsel with him as with a man wise in God. He suggested to me at the beginning to stay with him for two weeks or as long as I wished. Thus was I his guest for 24 years. Then he sent me to Maloyaroslavets where I have also been a guest for five years, and when I will return to my Fatherland (on high), God knows. In a similar manner you should arrange things for yourself. If one of your kinsfolk or someone close to your heart should become curious as to where you are planning to go, answer: "I am going away to improve my poor health at some warm spring." "When do you intend to return?" "As soon as my health improves." Hence, if you did not like the desert life (may God spare you), you could return home as the young lady that left without any regrets and you would not have to hear from ill-intentioned people the slightest personal criticism.

Forgive me for my wordiness and accept my assurance that I always pray to the Lord God for the salvation of your soul, that He would send you—as He did to Tobias—a guardian angel, so that you would be guided along the straight path to the quiet haven equal to that of the angels, the monastic life.

April 13th, 1844.

THE PEACE OF GOD
Letter 182

My heart rejoices, and I thank God Who has bestowed peace upon your heart and inclined it to His Holy Will, and I ask you to accept both the pleasant and unpleasant, which I hope shall cause God's peace to dwell in your heart. Then a dark, narrow and damp cell will be as consoling to you as a bright and beautiful palace. You look on your fellow laborers, your sisters in the Lord who have dry and well-lit cells, but if the peace of God does not dwell in their souls will not they, even more than you who have no shelter, be forever without peace? Thus, the cause of your disturbance comes not from your cell but from the adversary who envies the good effect of your soul's disposition. You saw what bright and spacious cells I have, but I would gladly change them for a damp cellar ... such, however, is not the will of God. So let us together cast our care upon the Lord and submit to His Holy Will. I rejoice and glorify God that my sinful words have wrought a good impression. Whoever with faith asks someone and fervently carries out what he hears, that one has heard the Lord, according to His testimony: *He that heareth you heareth Me* (Luke 10:16). Therefore thanksgiving should be offered not to the instrument who uttered the words, but solely to the Lord God, Who sometimes makes His will known through us sinners.

June 15, 1841.

P.S. Your attached letter to the honorable M.N. I will deliver when I am at home, and I will not refuse to talk with her when she asks questions. But without any questions it is not easy to begin, for as it is written: *Ask thy father and he will declare unto thee; thine elders, and they will tell thee* (Deut. 32:9). I spoke much with K. and everything is covered. But M.N. didn't ask me a single question and therefore I had nothing to say to her.

SEEKING SPIRITUAL BENEFIT WITH HUMILITY
Letter 188

You write that you don't get as much benefit from Moscow priests as from priests in hermitages. This can be because *a prophet is not without honor, save in his own country* (Matt. 14:57), nor is he trusted. Therefore, it is not they [the Moscow priests] who are guilty, but those who seek spiritual profit without faith. There are humble people who are able to assimilate something beneficial from every priest, and there are people who are not humble, who not only do not entirely trust living priests, but do not even have faith in the departed Fathers, glorified by the Church. Therefore I fervently wish that you, a sincere follower, would be as the first, and not the second, so that the Lord might look also upon your humility, and you would need neither to go into the desert nor to Jerusalem. For the Kingdom of God is not on a high mountain, but on earth below, since those of a humble heart shall find it within themselves. May the Lord God grant all of us to find such great treasure by His grace, and by the prayers of the Theotokos and all of the saints.

December 8th, 1840.

VOLUNTARY OBEDIENCE
Letter 190

I am consoled by your present manner of life, by which you are following others into the Kingdom of Heaven. I greet you with the holy Fast and with your approaching nameday. I ask you to accept the enclosed booklet of St. Maximus, *On Love,* so that you might teach us to love one another voluntarily and not out of necessity. For he who abides in love abides in God, and God abides in that man. In order to submit voluntarily to what is good, make an effort for this purpose to read the Epistle of

ELDER ANTHONY OF OPTINA

the holy Apostle Paul to the Hebrews, the final section [Heb. 13:17-21] which, with God's help, will give you an understanding of how to obey voluntarily and not out of compulsion.

November 13th, 1850

TEMPTATION AND HUMILITY
Letter 193

I read your letter and see that your soul is full of the most bitter confusion, finding neither consolation nor rest. But you have not expressed it. What is the nature of this powerful temptation that has befallen you, that the pen cannot describe what your soul has experienced? Therefore I did not feel comfortable replying to your speechless explanation. Not long ago I read in the book of St. Isaac the Syrian in Homily 36 [Homily 60 in English edition], where it says: "It is not God's good pleasure that those whom He loves should live in ease while they are in the flesh. He wishes them rather, so long as they are in this life, to abide in affliction, in oppression, in weariness, in poverty, in nakedness, isolation, illness, far from relatives and in sorrowful thoughts, and so forth.... For God knows that it is impossible for those who live in bodily ease to hold firmly to His love, and therefore He restrains them from ease and its enjoyment"*

If a temptation has occurred to incite you against your mother who received you at the tonsure, then I tell you that this is the heaviest trial, and there can be none heavier. But your impatience and lack of skill in relationships are to blame. When you learn to see the face of Christ in the face of your sponsor at the monastic tonsure , then you will be reverent before her, will

---

* *The Ascetical Homilies of St. Isaac the Syrian* (Brookline, Massachusetts: Holy Transfiguration Monastery, 1984), pp. 293-294.

love her and obey her in all things. Without this feeling, you run to her, thinking little whether you have come at the right time. Is Matushka resting? Is she perhaps praying, is she reading? Is she not busy with some necessary monastic duty? If Matushka says to you, "Come later, my dear, I can't speak with you now," then, downcast, you leave dissatisfied to your cell. There you take up paper and pen and write two or three pages of various explanations, in a murmuring spirit and in dissatisfaction at various things, and ask Matushka to read all this and console you. Your explanation shows more brazenness than the humility of Christ. If it were to continue forever like this, then your soul could never be peaceful. Although you live in that quiet haven, you would be, as it were, amidst a storm at sea, ever storm-tossed and choking in your tears. May the Lord God preserve you from such a fate and may He help you to make a good beginning. Above all may the Lord grant you the fervent desire to acquire true humility, which abides not in words but in the heart. It is acquired by the unceasing remembrance of one's sins and one's unworthiness, and by trying not to be meddlesome. According to the teaching of St. Isaac the Syrian: "Just as salt is necessary for any food, so too, humility is necessary for every virtue. Humility will present one before God even without good deeds, and without it all our good deeds are in vain.... Haste cannot be found in a humble man, nor bustle, light-mindedness and confusion, but he abides at all times in silence and in rest."* Therefore if you love to see good days, love holy humility with your whole soul and you will rest in the Lord.

September 6th, 1855.

---

* Homilies 69 and 71.

THE FAULTS OF OTHERS
Letter 196

First, by these meager lines I offer you my respectful thanks for the hospitality and repose you offered me, a wanderer.

Allow me to inform you as to what I have noticed about you—namely, that the restlessness of your spirit does not at all proceed from a damp cell, but from an accumulation of sins, as St. David says: *There is no peace in my bones in the face of my sins* (Psalm 37:3). The second is the most important—when we, according to the word of Christ, are *meek and lowly in heart,* then we *shall find rest unto* our *souls* (Matt. 11:28-29). Is this not true? Glory be to God that your cell is one such as the righteous Lazarus, who lay before the gates [of the rich man's house], never had (See Luke 16:20). Therefore you should thank God from the depth of your soul that He has not recompensed you according to your sins.

Again I noticed in you and in others a lack of peace towards your Lady Abbess. This enmity is also incorrect, for there is no authority which is not of God—that is, God appoints for us both good and obstinate authorities, the first unto consolation, and the second to bring us to contrition and humility. For this reason the holy Apostle Peter counsels us to obey our masters, not only the good and the meek, but the obstinate, too. *For this,* he says, *is thankworthy* (I Pet. 2:19). Skill is needed on our part so that when we come together we will not have prejudiced conversations about the faults of our superiors. For a wicked heart usually meditates wicked things and makes known wicked things, as St. John of the Ladder says: "God darkens the eyes of skilled novices before the defects of their superiors, but enlightens them concerning their virtues. The devil acts on the contrary: he blinds the eyes of unskilled novices to the virtues of their superiors so that they will not see anything good in them, but before their shortcomings and failings he renders them bright so that not a single defect escapes them."* Therefore, good mother, watch your heart against enmity and judgment, so that the grace of God does not depart from you. What are the sins of others to us, when we are up to our ears in endless sins. Let us henceforth pray and entreat God: *Set, O Lord, a watch before my mouth. Incline not,* O Lord, *my heart unto words of evil. O Lord, turn away mine eyes, so that I do not see* the failings of my superiors! (Ps. 140:3,4; Ps. 118:37). O Lord, grant me to see my own failings!

August 31, 1841.

P.S. To our dearest benefactress M.N. I ask you to bear witness of my high regard for her and to inform her that one earthly wanderer said that she was intending to move to another monastery, but I don't know if this is true or not. A holy Elder said that it is more profitable to change oneself than to change monasteries. For your monastery stands on the Lord's earth and under the protection of the Mother of God. What more could one ask?

MONASTIC GUIDELINES
Letter 206

To Christ's new novice N.

Answers to her questions:

1) Don't surrender yourself to the captivity of despondency and sloth, but repel them with the brief prayer: "O Lord Jesus Christ, Son of God, have mercy on me, a sinner."

2) You must see the face of God in the face of your superior and have devotion and all trust toward her; and if she makes

---

* Cf. Step 4:98

known all your weaknesses to others or orders you to do so, then for this very thing the Lord God will save you.

3) Pride loves to exercise superiority over others, but humility does not compare itself with anyone, reckoning itself to be worse than all.

4) Devoting yourself wholly to God you must not become disturbed about rags [clothing] nor let your heart become attached to them.

5) You must always go to the refectory, except in case of infirmity, during which times eat with a blessing in your cell.

6) (Concerning conduct with the sisters.) Have respect for them and love in the Lord, keeping yourself from engaging in idle talk and blasphemy.

7) (Concerning reproaches.) All types of reproaches may be directed at you, but you must not become angry, or you will thereby show the one bearing the reproaches to be worse than the offenders.

8) For the proud, criticism is a sharp knife; for the humble—a rich find.

9) (Concerning unprofitable conversations.) One must follow the example of St. David: *Like a deaf man I heard them not, and was as a speechless man that openeth not his mouth* (Ps. 37:13).

10) The One God acts in all confessors and elders; according to your faith in them will your questions be answered by them.

11) Perceptible profit to your soul is found in that which happens not according to your will.

12) In such instances one must say: *It is good for me,* O Lord, *that Thou hast humbled* my proud and sinful self (cf. Ps. 118:70).

13) (Concerning the one with whom you share a cell.) Regard her with sincere love, not as a senior but as your own mother, and what she does not approve, do not do.

14) Everything that is done out of holy obedience must leave one without disturbance, for holy obedience is above every rule and is greater than prayer and fasting.

15) *My child, if thou come to serve the Lord God, then prepare your soul for temptation* (Sirach 2:1), remembering the word of the Apostle: *They that are Christ's have crucified the flesh with the affections and lusts* (Gal. 5:24).

And so: Save yourself in the Lord and remember me, a sinner, in your prayers before God.

No date

ENDURING ALL THINGS
Letter 207

To the Novice of Christ N.N.

For permanent remembrance:

No matter what kind of bitterness befalls you, no matter what unpleasantness happens to you, say: "I will endure this for Jesus Christ!" Just say this and it will be easier for you. For the name of Jesus Christ is powerful—in His presence all unpleasant events are quelled, demons vanish, your annoyance will abate and your faintheartedness will be set at ease when you repeat His sweetest name. O Lord! grant me patience, courage and meekness! O Lord! grant me to see my own sins and not to judge anyone! It is profitable to frequently read the 20th Homily of St. Isaac the Syrian, which will heal your faintheartedness.

No date

Letter 208

To Christ's Beloved Novice N.N.

Friendly Advice in Prayerful Remembrance:*

1) When you rise from sleep, your first thought should be of God, your first word should be a prayer to God—your Father and Creator.

2) Bow down and offer thanksgiving to God Who did not let you perish with your iniquities.

3) Make a beginning to do what is best. For no one shall complete the path to heaven save he who begins every day well.

4) From the morning be a seraph in prayer, a cherub in actions and an angel in conduct.

5) Do not waste your time in idleness.

6) In all your deeds, words and thoughts have your mind in God.

7) Let your speech be quiet, humble, honorable and profitable. Silence enables you to use the words you want to say with discrimination, but *let no* idle or *corrupt communication proceed out of your mouth* (Eph. 4:29).

8) If laughter occurs, let it be only a smile and that not often.

9) Flee disputations and quarrels.

10) Love humility in everything and be not proud in anything.

11) Do not envy anyone in anything.

12) In food and drink observe restraint and do not be a sweet-tooth.

13) Be condescending in everything, and God will bless you and good people will praise you.

---

* Based on the Writings of St. Demetrius of Rostov.

14) Death is an end to all things, and one should always keep it in mind.

Such deeds as these will be as pleasing to the merciful Lord God as fragrant incense.

15) I ask you to remember, in your prayers to God, the unworthy monk Anthony, greatly sinful before everyone and before you, for which may the Lord God remember you in His Kingdom.

July 22nd, 1852.

PRAYER
Letter 222

According to your wish I am sending you a prayer rope for use in your cell. Pray fervently to the Lord God and your cold heart will be warmed by His sweetest name, for our God is fire. This cry destroys impure dreams and warms the heart for all His commandments. For this reason the prayerful calling upon His sweetest name must be the breath of our soul, must be more frequent than the beating of our heart.

February 14th, 1843.

HUMILITY, SILENCE AND PATIENCE
Letter 229

Much-ailing passion-bearer of Christ!

Seeing that you are constantly falling beneath the weight of your cross, I am afflicted in heart and ask the Lord God to help and assist you. During my first year of monastic life, I, like you, was bored daily and grew fainthearted. A thousand times I mentally consented to turn back but I was restrained by Christ's word: *No man having put his hand to the plough and looking back is fit for the Kingdom of God* (Luke 9:62). Desperately not wanting to perish, I resolved that it was better *to suffer affliction with the people of God* (Heb. 11:25) *than to dwell in the tents of sinners* (Ps. 83:11) and console myself with all kinds of worldly pleasures. Therefore, I think you will see the Lord's mercy upon you and will no longer feel despondency.

I ask you to put off your journey for the present time because one must seek the Kingdom of God not outside of oneself but within—that is, in one's own heart. Question: What is the Kingdom of God? Answer: The Kingdom of God is a virtuous life in God—to possess one's soul in humility, silence and patience. Abiding thus, you will see God's peace within yourself—that is, the Kingdom of God—and will find yourself in God's Kingdom after your repose.

September 14th, 1851.

ELDER ZOSIMA
Letter 309*

To the Beloved of God among Abbesses Mother Vera!

By means of these meager lines I offer you, dearest Matushka, from the depths of my soul, the most heart-rending thanks for your letter which pleased me exceedingly, and for the book sent together with it: the Life of your God-beloved Elder, the Venerable Father Zosima and his divinely-wise sayings.** For your zeal towards my lowliness may the Lord God grant you

---

* Written to Abbess Vera Verkhovsky, niece and disciple of Elder Zosima of Siberia.

** Originally published in Russian under the title *The Life and Labors of the Reposed in the Lord Elder of Blessed Memory, Schemamonk Zosima*, Moscow, 1889. Reprinted by the St. Herman of Alaska Brotherhood, Platina, California, 1977. English translation was published as *Elder Zosima: Hesychast of Siberia* by Abbess Vera Verkhovsky (St. Herman of Alaska Brotherhood, 1990).

His mercy! The publication of this book will be of great benefit to the many who will read it, especially to those living the monastic life. For its second publication I advise you to supplement it with something edifying from the life of Mother M. With the third edition of this edifying book I ask you to be so obedient, my Matushka, as to add something from your own life to the glory of God and the profit of those who will read it, and to the eternal memory of yourself. If you disregard this it will be a sin upon your soul, for this is not vainglory.

With this I, the lowly one, attach the five books of St. Isaiah the Solitary,* which I am sending out of my sincere love towards you in Christ Jesus, for from my soul I honor you and have reverence toward your God-beloved person.

May 18th, 1860.

---

* Published in 1860, these books were newly published when Elder Anthony sent this letter.

The main Optina Monastery Church of the Entry of the
Theotokos, as it looks today after its restoration.

APPENDICES

ОПТИНА-ПУСТЫНЬ. Видъ Храмовъ и колокольни съ восточной стороны

Optina Monastery as it looked before the Revolution—inside view.

I

A Letter of
Abbot Anthony Bochkov

*August 24th, 1865,
to a monk of Optina Monastery (written after receiving
news of the repose of Abbot Anthony Putilov).*

YOUR LETTER brought me joy although in it there were
tidings of death. Today I asked N.P. about you in a letter:
whether all the Optina fathers were still alive. Having written
this question to you in the morning, I received towards evening
your reply for which I am very grateful. I will say a few words
about the newly reposed Abbot Anthony, with whom I lived
nearly a year in the Skete in the same building.

Fr. Anthony was a true son of our Mother, the Orthodox
Church, a strict fulfiller of all her commandments and even
counsels, a profound authority and guardian of her rules and
traditions. By his entire life he proved that monasticism is
possible in our time and that Christ's commandments are not
grievous. He was a eunuch in spirit who, abandoning all his
possessions, followed Christ, taking up his cross, and by inner
discretion *mortifying his members* (Col. 3:5) for the sake of the
Kingdom of God. From desert-dwelling, from standing and
prostrations, and partially from sickness (which he likewise

contracted from the dense and swampy forests of the Smolensk Province), his legs turned into single open wounds, involuntarily reminding one of the wounds of Christ.

In his youth he was tested by the Lord by means of an unusual trial; he was placed like gold in a furnace. This great furnace was Moscow in flames in 1812. Fr. Anthony, with a few compatriots, remained, as if offered as a sacrifice together with our ancient capital, the Russian Jerusalem. A virgin youth in this Babylonian furnace, accounted worthy because of his purity to be numbered with the youths of Chaldea, he was strengthened in faith in God's Providence, which leads His beloved from despair to the cherished rest of stillness. He, like a captive, bore on his shoulders a heavy *paramon*—the knives of the adversaries—and humbly bowed his neck beneath this difficult yoke placed on all Russia for a season by the Right Hand of the Most High.

Then he came to live in the desert, and later moved into your forests, where with his brother he was the first bee of your Skete hive, a gatherer and worker of that fragrant honey and honeycomb which afterwards sweetened our parched throats. From that time on, the beautiful flowers of monasticism grew in your Monastery and until now adorn her. Then, after a short obedience as abbot, he moved on to his suffering, ailing retirement which was crowned, as you have written, by a joyful, monastic death.

The late Fr. Anthony was a true bloodless martyr of obedience. Being obedient in everything to his older brother, Elder and Abbot [Moses], abasing himself and his personality, being but a fulfiller of the directives of his father-brother, he, nonetheless, involuntarily shone with his God-given and abundant talents. An outstanding reader and singer, one of the best leaders of the Divine services of all monasticism, he was the first adornment of Optina, especially of the Skete church, which to him was his beloved and sole place of spiritual consolation, his first thought, his life. He kept order in the Skete church, her sacred ritual; he loved her beauty, her purity; he was ready with his lips to remove the slightest speck of dust that he might notice on the face of his beloved little church, which grew gradually during his time in its splendor and was first hewn by his axe. The services of the virgin Elder were true Divine services. Entirely given over to the Spirit-Comforter, from the moment when he first raised his hands until his departure from church, he did not belong to himself, but seemed reborn and joined with the Cherubim who are depicted mystically by their fiery and graceful ministry.

Leaving church for his quiet life in his cell, he became again the first servant of his older brother, a hesychast out of love for and with the blessing of his father. Obedience compelled him against his own nature to accept for a time the abbacy of the Maloyaroslavets Monastery. But, torn from the hive of the Skete, and an ascetic by the inclination of his heart, he was simply exhausted by this obedience. (I will not begin to say how difficult it was!) Then with joy he returned to his dear monastery, and, of course, walled himself off, just as in my time, with whole walls of patristic books, from every temptation except disease. I have not known such a lover of reading as the late Fr. Anthony. Conversation with the saints who have gone on before us was always for him a preferred way of passing his time, which for many seems to drag on so heavily and for so long, but for him, in view of his natural joviality, passed unnoticeably during the monotonous Skete life of my time. I can say that in light of his strictness to himself, by attentiveness and the guarding of the lips, he sometimes was able with a light, kind joke to evoke a smile now and then from those closest to him. This joke, like an unexpected spark or a flash of light on a dark monastic mantle, would immediately die away. During my time (almost thirty years ago) he had few disciples. Sabbatius, devoted to him with his whole soul, alone was his cell-attendant and looked after the unacquisitive Elder. One will find few like Sabbatius with such faithfulness and devotion.

Forgive me, that I haven't preserved more reminiscences of the short time of my stay with the reposed Elder. Whatever came into my head I have sent to your attention like a leaf that has withered and breathed its last, preserved for thirty years between the pages of a forgotten book.

2

An Amazing Incident

WHICH TOOK PLACE AFTER THE
DEATH OF ABBOT ANTHONY

On October 26th, 1866, a spiritual daughter of Abbot Anthony, the woman landowner E. S., while returning home from a visit and crossing the deep river Protva, almost next to her own home, fell with the carriage and coachman and horses from the ferry into the water. The carriage with the woman went to the bottom; the coachman, standing on the wheels, was only able to get his head above water. Some of the horses went down, others swam free, but the woman E. S. with the carriage didn't appear after the plunge into the water. Finding herself underwater and knowing her frightful predicament, E. S., covering her face with a shawl, turned to prayer, but for a long time there was no help; the water covered her more with every passing moment. She began to experience cramps from the cold and the strongest pain appeared in her chest, for the water began to force its way inside through her mouth. At the same time, she saw before her mind's eye all her children. E. S. reckoned all this as the harbinger of her approaching death and she was already despairing of life, but a certain awareness remained. She remembered Fr. Anthony and thought: "Batiushka! I always besought you that I might have a Christian death and now I am dying without repentance." In that instant it seemed to her that someone closed her mouth with something warm, and after that, she fell asleep.

When the news spread through the village that the woman had drowned and that no one had the resolve to pull her out, one kind peasant, who had found shelter in her home, left his work and hurried to help the woman who had drowned. Having found the carriage in the water with a board, and not having found the woman, he started to look for her on the bottom with a gaff hook. He found her and pulled her out without any signs of life; her heart was not beating and her pulse could not be felt. They carried the ashen E. S. off to her own home. Her clothing had frozen and there was no other way to take it off than to tear it to pieces. A priest was summoned and two doctors from the nearest town. A little while having passed, the priest, although he did not expect to receive an answer from the obviously dead woman, asked nonetheless: "Would E. S. like to partake of the Holy Mysteries?" To everyone's surprise she opened her eyes and said, "I would like to." She was immediately confessed and given the Holy Mysteries. With the doctors' aid she improved a little and with the passage of time she grew strong. E. S. is presently alive [1870].

3

An Entry from the Diary of Hieromonk Euthymius

FOR JANUARY 20TH, 1857

From the book Holy Things Under a Bushel *by Sergei Nilus, Holy Trinity-St. Sergius Lavra, 1911.*

January 20th. Sunday. Unfortunately for all my brothers in Christ, Archimandrite Moses did not serve because of his ailing legs; the wounds on his left leg had opened and sapped all his strength. It appears that the Lord still preserves monks such as Monk Dorotheus "of the mighty ascetic life" in the person of our Father Archimandrite [Moses] and his honorable brother in the flesh and in spirit, Abbot Anthony, and in those similar to them who secretly serve the Lord. The world knows them not and doesn't want to know them. We monks are their unworthy fellow travellers on the path to the Kingdom of the never-setting Light, and even we are rarely vouchsafed to learn during their lifetime what a propitious sacrifice for the sins of the world they offer to God by their hidden ascetic labors: vigils, fasts, standing at prayer, tears—by all the endless (like the human soul) and interior monastic labors, which are reflected in external ascetic feats. The sores on the legs of Archimandrite

Moses would open and hinder him in serving the Divine Liturgy. How did he contract these sores? When Father Archimandrite and his brother Abbot Anthony, leaving all the delights of the world for Christ's sake, went to dwell in the solitude of the dense, barely passable forests in the Roslavl district of the Smolensk Province, they added to their exploit of prayer the God-pleasing handicraft of copying sacred books—the books of the Divine Services, the Lives of the Saints and the great teachers of monasticism, the ancient ascetics. The time appointed for prayer they spent standing and they performed their handiwork standing as well, out of feelings of reverence for those great and glorious ones whose written works they copied for their cell use. Hence, excruciating sores developed on the legs of both brothers. This would have remained unknown to us, even to those closest to them, if the Lord had not glorified those who glorified Him, in order to edify us and strengthen us in faith and in ascetic struggles.

When Abbot Anthony governed the newly built Skete of our Monastery, amongst the number of the Skete brethren there was one monk of good moral disposition, but who suffered from a malady of passion for lack of rest at night, for which reason he often didn't come to the brotherhood's morning hymnody. In the Skete, Matins, as we have in the Monastery, is chanted at one or two o'clock in the morning. With the passage of time this habit became so rooted in the monk that he totally stopped getting up for Matins. At the same time, Fr. Anthony's affliction of the legs increased to such a degree that he couldn't put on his boots and, for this reason, he stopped going to the common services, carrying out his prayer rule in his cell. It seems that this monk, in justification of his lackadaisical attitude, or perhaps because of the enmity of the demons (who knows?), became so stubborn in his listlessness that when the monk assigned to awaken the brothers came to summon him to Matins in the Abbot's name, he refused to reply to the invitation. This was brought to the attention of Fr. Anthony who, of course, did not tarry in summoning the reprobate monk.

"What are you doing, skipping Matins?" asked the Skete Superior.

"Forgive my weakness, Batiushka, for God's sake," replied the monk. "But, I tell you truly, I can't get up so early. I'll carry everything out, I'll expend all my effort to shape up in every way, but this is beyond my strength. Would it really be pleasing to God, if, obeying you, I bore an obedience beyond my strength with grumbling, and, having borne it, on the following day were fit for nothing?"

With all his love and power of persuasion Fr. Anthony exhorted the stubborn brother, asked, begged, and tried to demonstrate that disobedience in one thing makes of no avail all amendment in the rest. But our monk would not be persuaded even if he had to leave the Skete for good. In what way did the Elder make him understand? The assigned monk continued to go awaken him, but the monk continued to sleep through Matins until a certain thing happened that broke the stubbornness of his hardened heart. One day Matins was being celebrated and the Abbot himself was present. The service ended, the brethren left the church and, after everyone, the Abbot walked out. He didn't go to his own cell but headed straight for the cell of that monk. He approached the door, said a prayer and entered the cell. The monk, seeing the Skete Superior, jumped from his bed frightened, but Fr. Anthony, in his mantle, fell on his knees before him:

"My brother, my brother who is perishing. I am responsible for you, for your soul, to give an answer before the Lord. You did not go to your holy obedience—I went for you. Have mercy, my brother, on yourself and on my sinful self!"

He spoke at the feet of his novice. He wept, and beneath his mantle there was a whole pool of blood. Blood had poured into his boots from the open sores on his legs while he had been standing and, when he bowed to the ground to his brother, it poured out as if out of a bucket.

Thus the great one saved his weak fellow soldier.

As long as such power of the spirit of Christ's love is concealed in the spiritual bosom of Russia, my holy land is still alive and will remain alive! Be merciful, O Lord, if this power grows scarce!…

Holy Father Anthony, pray to God for us!

+

TROPARION TO SAINT ANTHONY OF OPTINA
Tone 7

O desert-dweller of the forests of Roslavl,* beholding there uncreated Light of Mt. Tabor.* O holy builder of the Optina Skete with thy brother Moses,*acquiring therein wisdom not of this world.* O Father Anthony the meek at heart,* by thy prayers obtain for us thy wisdom of humility.

GLOSSARY

akathist: a special group of hymns of praise to our Lord Jesus Christ, the Mother of God, or a saint, sung standing. (The word is derived from the Greek "not sitting.")

antidoron: the loaves remaining from the Proskomedia after the piece which is to become the Body of Christ has been cut out; these loaves are cut up and distributed to the faithful at the end of the Liturgy. (The word is derived from the Greek "instead of the Gifts.")

batiushka: an endearing term for a priest, meaning "little father."

cliros: the place in church from where the readers and the choir read and chant the service.

epitrachelion: a vestment which hangs from the neck of the priest and is the one indispensable vestment for all priestly ministrations.

hesychast: someone who lives the "quiet" life, in seclusion from the world, and who devotes himself entirely to God by means of the Jesus Prayer with a heart burning with love for God.

hierodeacon: a monk who is ordained a deacon.

hieromonk: a monk who is ordained a priest.

horologion: the "Book of Hours," i.e., the service book containing the psalms, hymns and prayers chanted each day which comprise the basic structure of the daily cycle of services—Vespers, Nocturnes, Matins, First Hour, Third Hour, Sixth Hour, and Ninth Hour.

kamilavka (pl. *kamilavki*): the black cylindrical head covering worn by a monastic, with a black veil hanging behind.

kontakion: a hymn used in the daily cycle of services and also at Divine Liturgy in honor of a particular saint or feast, similar to a troparion.

lampada: an oil lamp hanging before an icon.

litia: a procession and solemn intercession at Vespers for special feasts, which takes place in the narthex of the church. Also, the shortened Office of the Dead which can be sung at the end of Divine Liturgy.

moleben: a prayer service in which the faithful ask for heavenly help or give thanks to God.

panikhida: a prayer service for those who have reposed.

paramon: a square piece of cloth with a cross and the words "I bear on my body the wounds of Christ" embroidered on it, worn by tonsured monks and nuns.

phelonion: the large stiff vestment worn by a priest at certain times in the daily cycle of services and also in Divine Liturgy.

podrasnik: a cassock worn by all monastics, including novices.

prosphoron (pl. *prosphora*): a small round loaf of bread prepared especially for the Divine Liturgy.

proskomedia: the service of preparation for the Divine Liturgy, during which, the "lamb" that is to become the Body of Christ is cut out of a prosphoron, and the living and the dead are commemorated.

schemamonk: one who has taken on the highest and strictest monastic discipline, leading a life of seclusion and prayer. He wears the "schema," a special cowl and stole.

Theotokos: the Greek word for the Mother of God; literally, "the God-birthgiver".

trapeza: the monastery refectory; also, the communal meal eaten in the refectory.

troparion: a hymn used in the daily cycle of services and also at Divine Liturgy in honor of a particular saint or feast.

typicon: the rules and orders governing the daily cycle of services and how they are typically served during the commemoration of saints and feasts. Also, the rule of life in a monastery.

INDEX

INDEX

INDEX

ELDER LEONID
OF OPTINA
by Fr. Clement Sederholm

Volume I in the Optina Elders Series:

ELDER LEONID
of Optina

by Fr. Clement Sederholm

Like a lion, Elder Leonid (†1841) introduced and firmly established in Optina the tradition of eldership as transmitted from St. Paisius Velichkovsky. Possessed with penetrating spiritual discernment, he was at the same time loving and fatherly, and thousands came to him to be healed both in soul and body.

272 pages, paperback, illustrated, $10.00 (ISBN 0-938635-50-6)

Order from: St. Herman Press, 10 Beegum Gorge Road
P. O. Box 70, Dept. EA, Platina, CA 96076

Silence

&

Solitude

Mystical Literature from the Christian East

St. Herman Press

ST. HERMAN OF ALASKA BROTHERHOOD

For three decades, the St. Herman Brotherhood has been publishing works of traditional spirituality.

Write for our free 80-page catalogue, featuring sixty titles of published and forthcoming books and magazines.

St. Herman Press
10 Beegum Gorge Road
P. O. Box 70, Dept. EA
Platina, CA 96076